THE COAST OF PUGET SOUND

THE COAST OF PUGET SOUND

ITS PROCESSES AND DEVELOPMENT

John Downing

A Washington Sea Grant Publication
Distributed by the University of Washington Press
Seattle and London

First published in 1983 by
Washington Sea Grant Program
University of Washington

Distributed by University of Washington Press
Seattle, Washington 98195

Publication of this book was supported by grants (04-5-158-48; 04-7-158-44021; NA79AA-D-00054; NA81AA-D-00030) from the National Oceanic and Atmospheric Administration and by funds from the Environmental Protection Agency. Writing and publication was conducted by the Washington Sea Grant Program under project A/PC-7.

Library of Congress Cataloging in Publication Data

Downing, John, 1946-
The Coast of Puget Sound.

(Puget Sound books)
Bibliography: p.
Includes index.
1. Coasts—Washington (State)—Puget Sound. II. Title.

II. Series.
GB458.8.D68 1983 551.4'57'097977 82-10961
ISBN 0-295-95944-4

for Mike, Elaine, and Kathy

Contents

Funds to support the publication of the Puget Sound Books were provided by the National Oceanic and Atmospheric Administration (NOAA) and by the Environmental Protection Agency (EPA)

About the Puget Sound Books

This book is one of a series of books that have been commissioned to provide readers with useful information about Puget Sound. . . .

About its physical properties—the shape and form of the Sound, the physical and chemical nature of its waters, and the interaction of these waters with the surrounding shorelines.

About the biological aspects of the Sound—the plankton that form the basis of its food chains; the fishes that swim in this inland sea; the regions marine birds and mammals; and the habitats that nourish and protect its wildlife.

About man's uses of the Sound—his harvest of finfish, shellfish and even seaweed; the transport of people and goods on these crowded waters; and the pursuit of recreation and esthetic fulfillment in this marine setting.

About man and his relationships to this region—the characteristics of the populations which surround Puget Sound; the governance of man's activities and the management of the region's natural resources; and finally, the historical uses of this magnificent resource—Puget Sound.

To produce these books has required more than six years and the dedicated efforts of more than one hundred people. This series was initiated in 1977 through a survey of several hundred potential readers with diverse and wide-ranging interests.

The collective preferences of these individuals became the standards against which the project staff and the editorial board determined the scope of each volume and decided upon the style and kind of presentation appropriate for the series.

In the Spring of 1978, a prospectus outlining these criteria and inviting expressions of interest in writing any one of the volumes was distributed to individuals, institutions, and organizations throughout Western Washington. The responses were gratifying. For each volume no fewer than two and as many as eight outlines were submitted for consideration by the staff and the editorial board. The authors who were subsequently chosen were selected not only for their expertise in a particular field but also for their ability to convey information in the manner requested.

Nevertheless, each book has a distinct flavor—the result of each author's style and demands of the subject being written about. Although each volume is part of a series, there has been little desire on the part of the staff to eliminate the individuality of each volume. Indeed, creative yet responsible expression has been encouraged.

This series would not have been undertaken without the substantial support of the Puget Sound Marine EcoSystems Analysis (MESA) Project within the Office of Oceanography and Marine Services/Ocean Assessment Division of the National Oceanic and Atmospheric Administration. From the start, the representatives of this office have supported the conceptual design of this series, the writing, and the production. Financial support for the project was also received from the Environmental Protection Agency and from the Washington Sea Grant Program. All these agencies have supported the series as part of their continuing efforts to provide information that is useful in assessing existing and potential environmental problems, stresses, and uses of Puget Sound.

Any major undertaking such as this series requires the efforts of a great many people. Only the names of those most closely associated with the Puget Sound Books—the writers, the editors, the illustrators and cartographers, the editorial board, the project's administrators and its sponsors—have been listed here. All these people—and many more—have contributed to this series, which is dedicated to the people who live, work, and play on and beside Puget Sound.

Alyn Duxbury and Patricia Peyton
July 1983

Preface

The scope and design of this book have undergone many alterations since its beginning more than four years ago. At the outset, the book was to present the state of oceanographical and geological knowledge of the coast of Puget Sound. The first order of business was necessarily to gather together all reports and studies of the subject. It became apparent to me, during this early phase, that the beaches and shoreline in the Pacific Northwest have not been studied as extensively as east coast and California beaches. Information sources were limited to regional inventories of coastal resources and studies of coastal engineering problems at a few specific sites, mostly in populated areas.

In order to be valuable to readers of diverse backgrounds and varied exposure to the subject, the scope of the book was expanded considerably. I decided that a major portion of it would cover some of the basic principles of sediment transport and wave effects on beaches. Although these principles are treated in other books, I have used examples of them taken exclusively from the shores of Puget Sound to show their regional significance. In addition to these introductory materials, a major chapter is devoted to engineering aspects of our beaches. This seemed an appropriate way to integrate existing oceanographic data with basic principles and to provide some practical guidelines for the interested property owner, planner, or developer. A spinoff of the expansion was that many more illustrations were included in the text. The added dimension of photographs, sketches, and graphs makes the subjects more comprehensible to those who best conceptualize ideas graphically. Text and illustrations work together to summarize existing information and to guide the reader to an understanding of the shore at most locations of the Sound whether or not they have been studied previously.

One of the reasons for reading a preface is to decide whether to read the book. This book is intended for a wide readership: it has information for the owners, present and future, of shore property; background data for engineers new to the area and unfamiliar with specific problems encountered by developers of Puget Sound shores; information for planners wishing to review coastal processes; and introductory level material for students of earth sciences.

The geographical scope of this book includes most of the inland marine coast of western Washington State with examples of coastal features drawn from a variety of locations in Puget Sound, Hood Canal, and the Strait of Juan de Fuca as well as from the San Juan Archipelago and the eastern Strait of Georgia. Most of the examples of coastal processes influenced by people, however, are concentrated in the populated areas about which more information is available. These geographical limitations underscore the need for continued study of our coast on a regional basis as begun in the early 1970s under programs supported by the Washington State Shoreline Management Act and the Federal Coastal Zone Management Act.

A brief note about terminology is in order. Some readers unfamiliar with oceanographic disciplines may perceive technical words as jargon and perhaps a nuisance. This perception may be somewhat justified, but in recent years it has become increasingly difficult to convey new information without using terms that are shorthand for complex ideas. In this volume, I have used a moderate number of technical terms because many readers will have prior exposure to the subject and for them these terms are a convenience. For others, most technical terms are briefly defined where they first appear in the text. A complete glossary is included as well, which will be useful for those who wish to pursue the more detailed accounts of case studies cited in the bibliography.

My personal interest in writing this book grew from research of a more technical nature into the mechanism of sand movement on open-ocean beaches. I was fascinated by the dynamics and ever-changing character of the shore and felt some responsibility to make its processes understandable to others. It is my hope that whatever your interests may be, the concepts of coastal processes and descriptions of the geological evolution of our shores will lead you to increased enjoyment, understanding, and appreciation of the Puget Sound region and its nearshore environment.

John Downing
July 1, 1983

Acknowledgments

It has been a great pleasure working with the many individuals who freely contributed both technical and personal support during the preparation of this book. My interest in beaches and coastal oceanography grew from many hours spent with Dick Sternberg, School of Oceanography, University of Washington, observing and discussing beaches along the West Coast. Dick has taught me much about the subjects in the book and without his guidance I could not have written it. Special thanks also go to Carolyn Threadgill for her editorial assistance and patience while we turned the manuscript into a book and to Kirk Johnson of Washington Sea Grant who helped me convey ideas better through pictures.

Michael Ruef of the Washington State Department of Ecology contributed much of the information about coastal hazards. The chapters on beach and coastal geology developed from the expert advice and considerable discourse with Ralph Keuler of the U.S. Geological Survey. Gilbert Bortleson and Robert Thorson, also of the USGS, provided interesting material and comments regarding historical shoreline changes and the glacial geology of Puget Sound. Eugene Richey and Jack Heavner of the Department of Civil Engineering, University of Washington, provided helpful guidance in the interpretation of the wave data provided by them and by Don Birrell, Fisheries and Environment Canada. Eric Nelson and Dave Schuldt, Navigation and Coastal Planning Division, U.S. Army Corps of Engineers, Seattle District, donated their time generously and provided access to open-file reports on many of the coastal engineering studies.

Finally, I extend my deepest appreciation to my family and close friends for the support and encouragement they provided while I wrote this book.

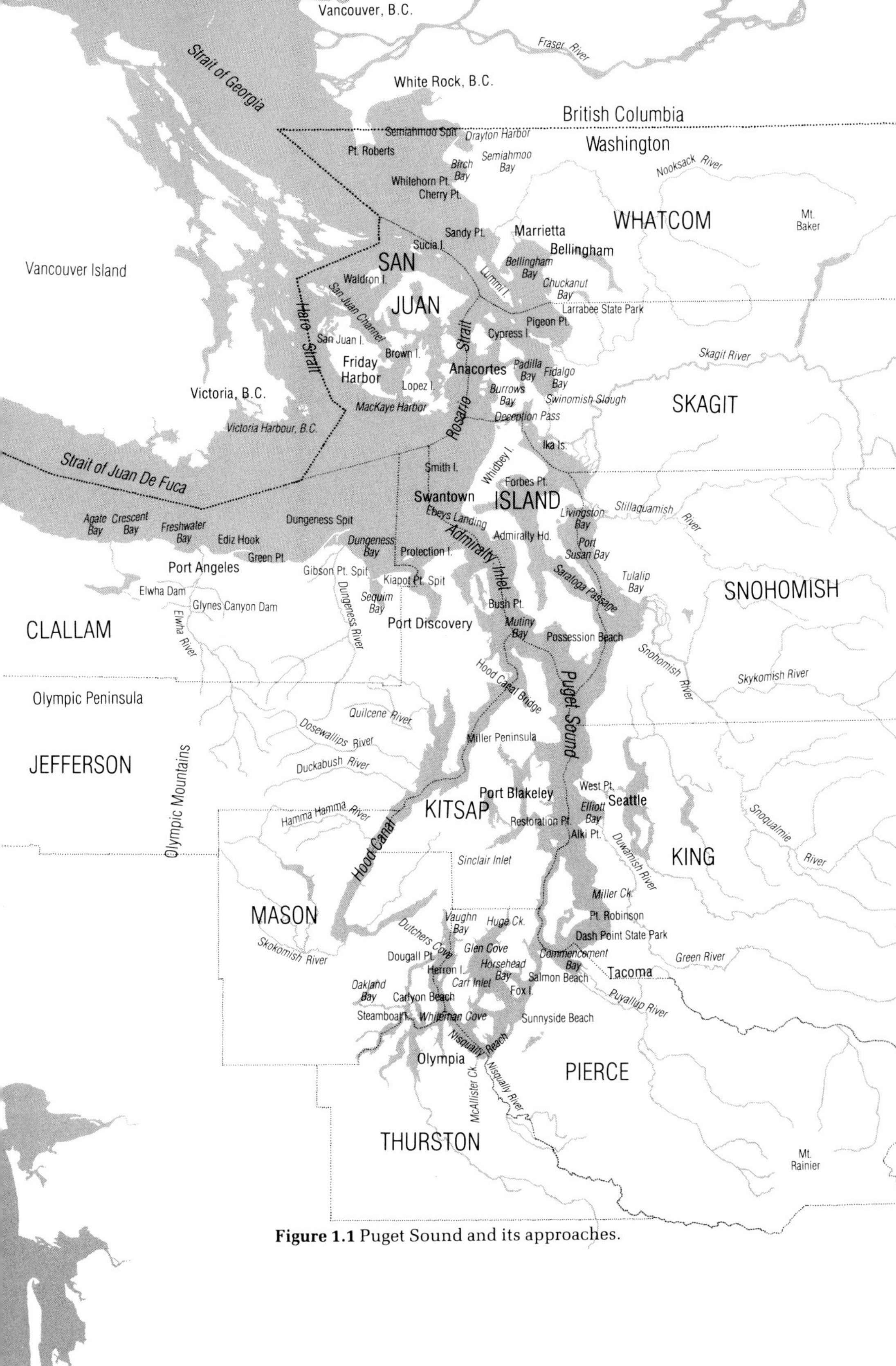

Figure 1.1 Puget Sound and its approaches.

CHAPTER 1

The Coastal Zone and Its Origin

The coast of Puget Sound and its adjacent inland waterways are natural phenomena which have a strong influence on the citizens of Washington. Much of the aesthetic and commercial value of this coast derives from the wide variety of physical resources it offers. These resources result from a complex sequence of geological events which began during the last Ice Age and continues to the present day. Among these events are at least two advances of glaciers into the Puget lowlands, with attendant oscillations in sea level, and the formation of several major rivers in the nearby Cascade and Olympic mountain ranges. Glaciation and the rivers of the region not only provided the sedimentary material necessary for beach formation along the coast, but established the natural trend of the nearly 3,220 kilometers (2,000 miles) of shoreline enjoyed today (Fig. 1.1).

Because of its rich geological legacy, Puget Sound displays most of the coastal features found worldwide in the temperate latitudes. The pattern and form of the coast vary greatly between the exposed shores of the Straits of Juan de Fuca and Georgia and the more sheltered areas of southern Puget Sound. Rock cliffs rising vertically more than 100 meters (328 feet) from breaking waves, broad tidal mud flats of imperceptible relief, and smooth sandy beaches all exist within a distance of fewer than 50 kilometers (30 miles).

The coastal features and resources of Puget Sound are best conserved and utilized through an understanding of their geological origins and the processes at work on the shore. Introduction of these subjects in the first chapters of this book follows a course that begins with regional processes associated with glaciation and river sedimentation and proceeds to more local ones resulting from the effects of waves, such as beach erosion and deposition. Against this background, the engineering aspects of coastal structures, hazards, and development are described to provide a practical view of coastal conditions as they exist today.

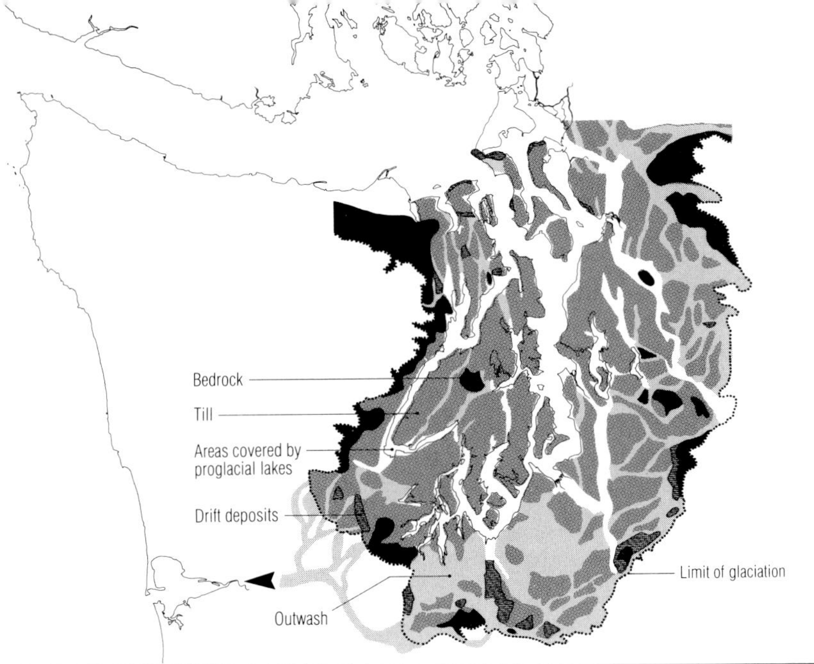

Figure 1.2 Glacial sediments in the Puget lowland. Till is most abundant and is a plentiful source of sand and gravel for beaches.

Glacial Legacies

Beaches, deltas, and other intertidal sedimentary features in Puget Sound acquired their forms and textures in very recent geological time, during the last 5,000 years. A considerably longer period, about 700,000–900,000 years, was required to complete events that provided the geographical setting and raw materials for the ongoing coastal evolution observable today. In essence, the sedimentary features on the shore are the finishing touches on a gigantic sediment movement project begun long ago by glacial ice.

Continental glaciers containing up to 10,000 cubic kilometers (2,383 cubic miles) of ice invaded the Puget lowland at least twice and probably four times during the Pleistocene Epoch. Two aspects of Pleistocene glaciation are of consequence to the evolution of coastal features. First, glacial ice excavated several long, narrow valleys during recurrent cycles of advance and retreat. These valleys, once filled with ice, now form Lake Washington, Lake Sammamish, Hood Canal, and the major basins of Puget Sound. Numerous smaller depressions also were scoured in bedrock by glacial ice. These form the many north–south oriented bays, inlets, and passages adjacent to the main basins of Puget Sound. The arrangement of the present shorelines was established 13,000 years ago when glacial ice retreated from the Puget lowland. At that time coastal marine processes had a place to begin.

The other constituent necessary for shore processes is a large amount of sediment. This was supplied in enormous quantities by each

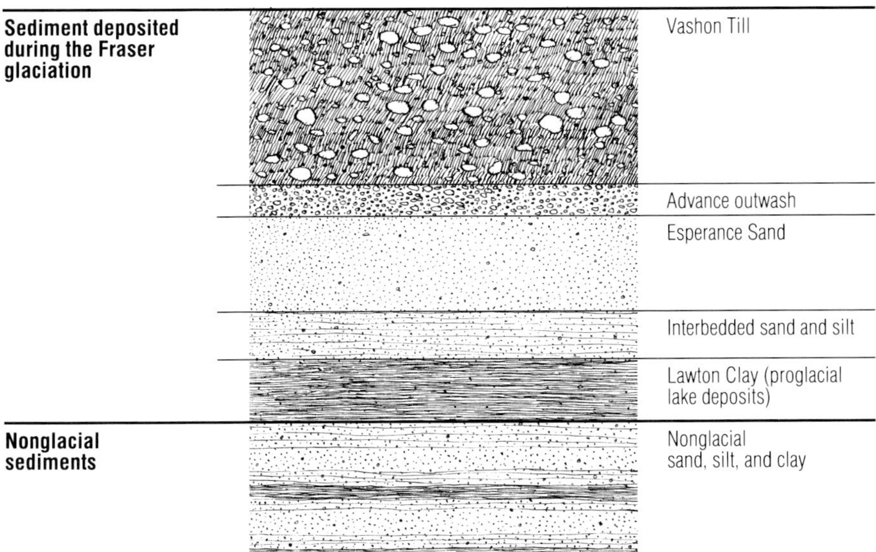

Figure 1.3 Glacial sediments of a coastal bluff. Vashon Till and advance outwash consist of mainly sand and gravel. Proglacial lake deposits are fine silts and clays.

cycle of Pleistocene glaciation. Figure 1.2 shows the extensive cover of till, outwash, and drift deposits emplaced by ice and meltwater streams in the Puget lowland during the last glaciation. These deposits are more than 100 meters (328 feet) thick at some locations and contain sediments of widely varying sizes. Most of the present coastal sedimentation around Puget Sound was directly affected by the last glaciation. In fact, large boulders and outcrops of glacial lake clay can be found together on the same beach at many sites in the Sound. The strata of glacial material are quite complex because of the variety of processes responsible for their deposition. Poorly sorted ice-deposited sediments with many grain sizes form the compact till deposits exposed at most shore bluffs (Fig. 1.3). Outwash sands and gravels deposited by streams that drained the ice sheet and laminated clay beds formed on lake bottoms at the edge of the glacier are also common in shore bluff strata. Because these strata were distributed irregularly and were deformed differently by ice loading after deposition, their mechanical strength, drainage capacity, slope stability, and resistance to processes that induce landslides vary widely from place to place.

Before waves and currents began to rework glacial deposits on the coast, two events associated with the retreat of the ice were completed. First, melting of a massive ice slab averaging 900 meters (2,950 feet) in thickness caused the earth's rocky crust under the Puget lowland to be uplifted. Uplift was completed about 6,000 years ago when the crust stabilized at its preglacial level. The amount of uplift varied in a nearly linear manner from zero near Tenino, Washington, the southern limit of the last glaciation, to about 140 meters (459 feet) in the vicinity of Whidbey Island. North of Whidbey Island the history of postglacial crustal movement is less clear.

Coincident with the uplift of the land surface, sea level was rising as melting glaciers around the world increased the volume of water in the oceans. To some degree these two events compensated each other but uplift occurred at about twice the rate of sea level rise until about 6,600 years ago. At that time the crust ceased to rise but the sea continued to do so until 5,000 years ago when it reached nearly the present level. Since 5,000 years ago, sea level has continued to rise but at a nearly imperceptible rate.

Precise water level measurements at sites around the world indicate that sea level in the ocean has risen at the average rate of about 1.0 to 1.2 millimeters (0.05 inch) per year during the last century. Because Puget Sound is located in a tectonically active part of the world, sea level is also affected by local vertical movements of the earth's crust. The influence of these effects is apparent in the long-term records of yearly average sea level for three locations in the Puget Sound area (Fig. 1.4). One would expect the increasing water volume in the oceans to affect these locations equally and yet the Neah Bay record shows a definite lowering trend of sea level not apparent at Seattle or Friday Harbor. This is due, in part, to vertical ground movements that have occurred unequally in the region.

Figure 1.4 summarizes sea level trends at other sites. If these trends alone were to determine the location of the coastline, at Seattle for example, the coastline could move from 2.43 meters (8 feet) to 12.2 meters (40 feet) landward in 100 years. Fluctuations of this order are significant to long-range plans in the coastal zone.

Beaches

The most prevalent coastal landforms to evolve from the last glaciation are the coarse sand and gravel beaches and high bluffs so common along the shores of Puget Sound. These beaches are a major subject of this book.

When used in conversation, the word beach invokes images of dry sand dunes and sunshine. Here, beaches are addresssed in a much broader sense to include the sediments in the narrow coastal zone that are influenced by wind waves and nearshore currents. Beaches develop along segments of the coast where there is a supply of unconsolidated (loose) sand and gravel that can be moved by waves. They include parts of the permanently submerged seabed beyond the lowest tides where sediment is agitated by wave action and extend to the landward limit of storm wave activity (Fig. 1.5). The features and condition of any par-

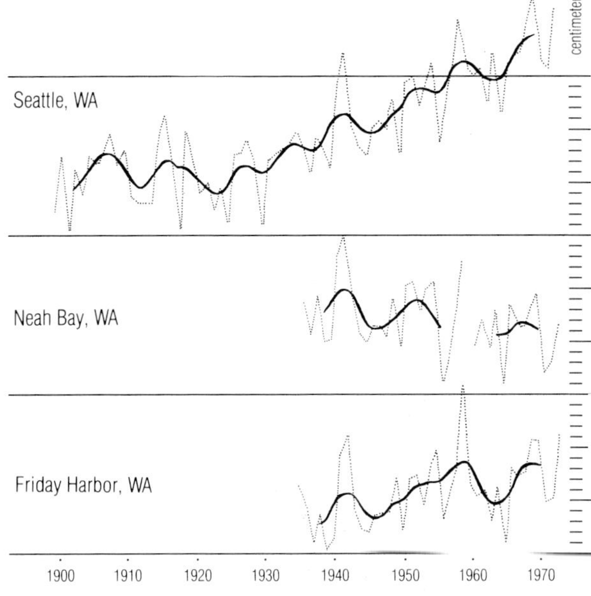

Figure 1.4 Long-term trends of sea level at three ports (solid lines). A slight drop of sea level at Neah Bay was probably caused by upward movement of the earth's crust. Dotted lines indicate fluctuations caused by oceanic conditions. Rates of sea level rise or fall (negative values) are given in the table below.

Port	Time Period	Trend (cm/century)
Seattle, WA	1899-1972 1935-1972	19.30[2] 21.34[1]
Neah Bay, WA	1935-1972	−13.58[1]
Friday Harbor, WA	1934-1972	2.28[1]
Vancouver, B.C.	1911-1979 1940-1979	−0.90[3] 6.40[3]
Victoria, B.C.	1910-1979 1940-1979	4.90[3] 2.70[3]

Rates of sea level rise and fall.

[1]Vanicek (1978)
[2]Hicks and Crosby (1974)
[3]Wigen and Stephenson (1979)

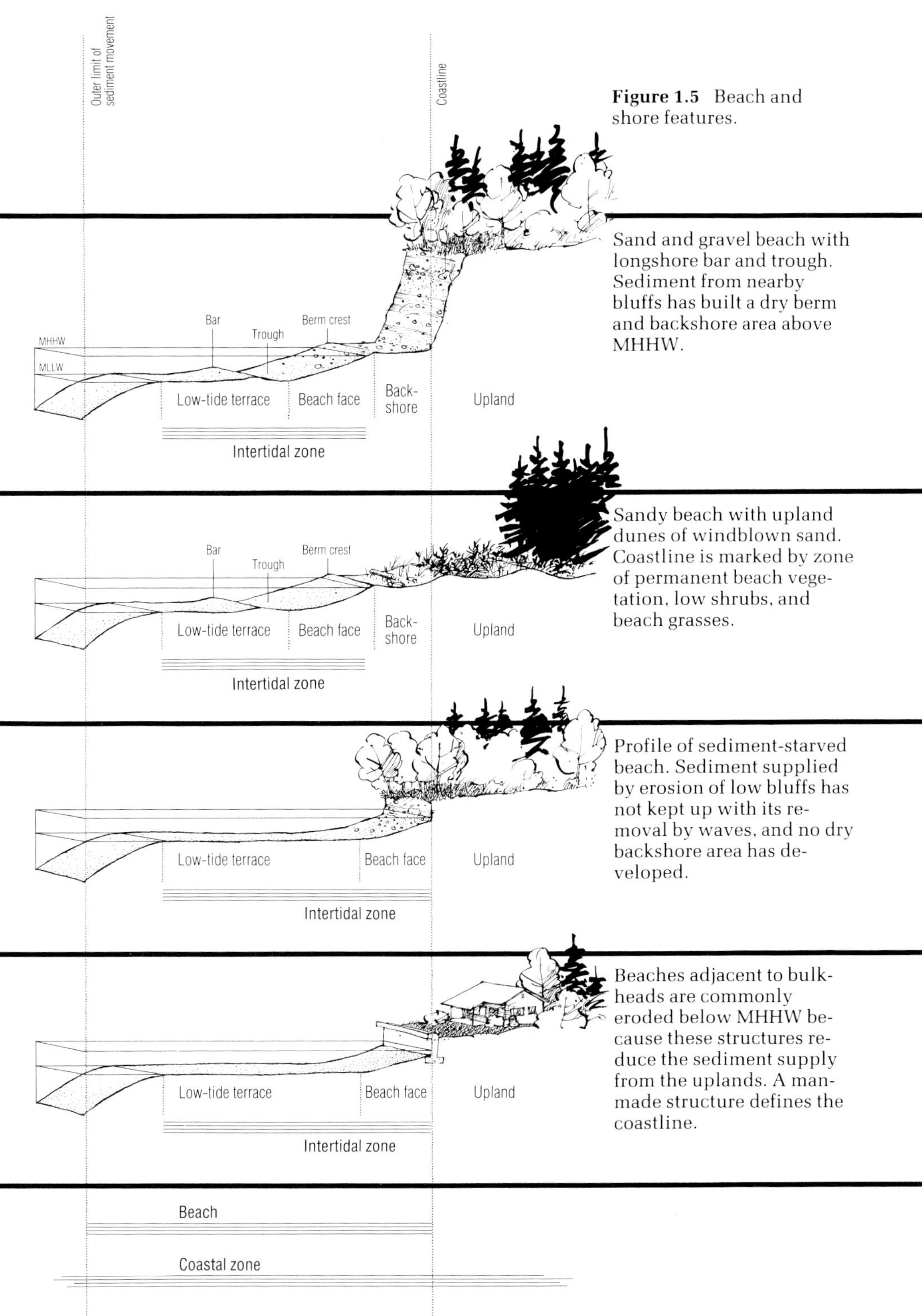

Figure 1.5 Beach and shore features.

Sand and gravel beach with longshore bar and trough. Sediment from nearby bluffs has built a dry berm and backshore area above MHHW.

Sandy beach with upland dunes of windblown sand. Coastline is marked by zone of permanent beach vegetation, low shrubs, and beach grasses.

Profile of sediment-starved beach. Sediment supplied by erosion of low bluffs has not kept up with its removal by waves, and no dry backshore area has developed.

Beaches adjacent to bulkheads are commonly eroded below MHHW because these structures reduce the sediment supply from the uplands. A man-made structure defines the coastline.

ticular beach are due to both the type of sediment and the balance between its supply and removal.

Figure 1.5 shows cross sections of beaches typical of shores along Puget Sound that are both exposed to moderate wave activity and adequately supplied with sediment. This area of the seabed and shore may appear to be loosely defined, particularly with regard to legal coastal boundaries, plat surveys, and the like. The geographical limits of the beach do, in fact, oscillate to and fro with the tide; seasonal cycles of winter storm erosion and summer growth of the beach can change the boundaries more dramatically. Such fluctuations cause some very difficult legal problems, but they also serve as a reminder that the beaches are dynamic systems where terrestrial and marine processes affect one another rather than stable geographical entities. More importantly, the beaches' constantly changing character keeps one's mind open to the wide variety of physical processes that continuously shape and rework most segments of the Puget Sound coast.

A beach consists of several parts; these include the backshore, beach face or foreshore, and low-tide terrace (Fig. 1.5). The backshore is the portion of the beach that remains dry except during severe storms. It is the most highly valued part of the beach for recreational uses as well as a natural barrier protecting the uplands from wave attack. Unfortunately, this resource is in very short supply on the sand-starved beaches of Puget Sound and permanent backshores exist along only 32 percent of the shoreline.

The berm is the flat-topped portion of the backshore where sediments accumulate when water from wave runup percolates into the beach. Several berms of various sizes can form on a beach (Fig. 1.6). Each berm crest marks the upper limit of wave runup during a time when similar-sized waves prevailed for one or perhaps several successive high tides. Large berms, located high on the beach, are formed by storm waves which occur during a high spring tide. Such berms are composed of coarse sediment and logs, not easily moved by small waves, and can persist for several years before being eroded by a storm. Smaller berms such as the ones lower down on the beach face are ephemeral features and may persist for only a few days.

The sloped part immediately seaward of the berm crest is called the beach face or foreshore. Wave forces are the most intense in this region, and the beach face is continually modified through active sediment movement as the tide rises and falls. The upper limit of sediment-starved beaches may be below mean higher high water where beach sediments rest against the base of a bluff or bulkhead (Fig. 1.5). Where longshore transport to a beach is blocked, the beach is eroded and develops a flat, low angle profile. The beaches at Swantown and Mutiny Bay, for example, are both sandy but the Swantown site was eroded just before the photograph was taken (Fig. 1.7).

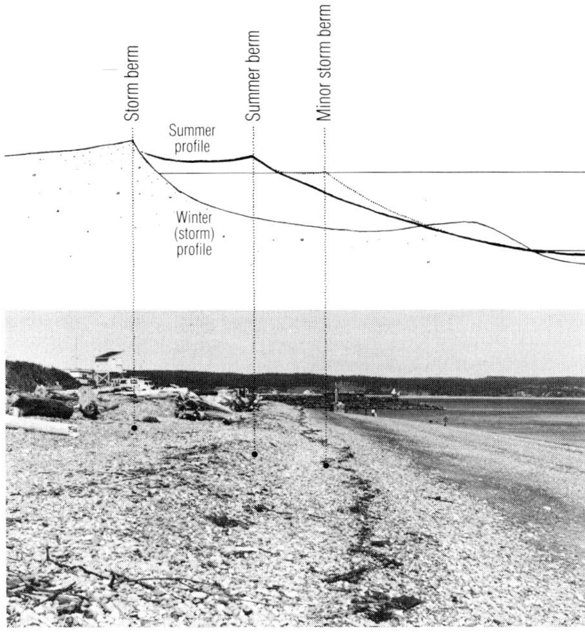

Figure 1.6 Winter and summer profiles of a beach showing berms formed by changing wave activity. Sand moved offshore by large winter waves is returned by smaller waves to rebuild the beach in summer.

Figure 1.7 Sandy beach with flat gently sloping profile at Swantown, a site on the west shore of Whidbey Island exposed to large waves.

Steep beach face and wide backshore at Mutiny Bay, Whidbey Island, a more sheltered site with a steady supply of sand.

Seaward of the beach face a broad platform, called the low-tide terrace, extends out to about mean lower low water (MLLW). On most shores of the Sound the low-tide terrace consists of sandbars formed by nearshore currents and the continuous oscillatory water movement produced by waves. These bars are a reservoir for sediment in transit along the shore. Storage occurs here even when the upper part of the beach is starved of sand and gravel. In making beach observations it should be realized that all of the features described above will not exist on an individual beach. For instance, only the coastline is obvious on a beachless rocky shore. Furthermore, the size of a particular feature will vary from one beach to another. An experienced beach observer notes the presence of all features, regardless of their size, as they each provide clues about the present condition and future stability of the beach.

The seaward limit of a beach varies in relation to the bottom sediment characteristics (sand, pebbles, cobbles, and so forth) and the size of the waves breaking on the shore. On exposed shores of Puget Sound beaches can extend out to a depth of approximately 10 meters (33 feet); but along sheltered bays and passes where wind wave growth is limited they may extend out to water depths of only 2 to 3 meters (6–10 feet). At some distance beyond the intertidal zone, the water is sufficiently deep that the sediment is rarely moved by waves alone. In protected bays, where small waves move sediment at depths only a few tens of centimeters below mean lower low water, beaches occupy just the intertidal zone. Along the western shore of Dungeness Spit, however, the beach is of much wider extent since large storm waves move sediment at much greater depths and throw it far up on the shore.

The landward limit of the beach is called the coastline; it divides the region dominated by marine processes (waves and currents) from the region influenced by terrestrial processes. Waves and currents do not directly affect land stability or the quality of ground and surface waters beyond the coastline. Around Puget Sound it is commonly marked by a cliff or upland sedimentary deposit formed during the last glaciation (i.e., geological process, Fig. 1.5). The coastline may also be marked by the seaward edge of a dune field, permanent vegetation, or a man-made boundary such as a seawall. The upland area landward of the coastline can be included as part of the coastal zone. Uplands are the landforms near the shore (including islands and sea stacks) which are located above the highest water level likely to occur in 50 to 100 years.

Figure 1.8 Coastal features formed by sediment deposition—deltas, tidal flats, and spits.

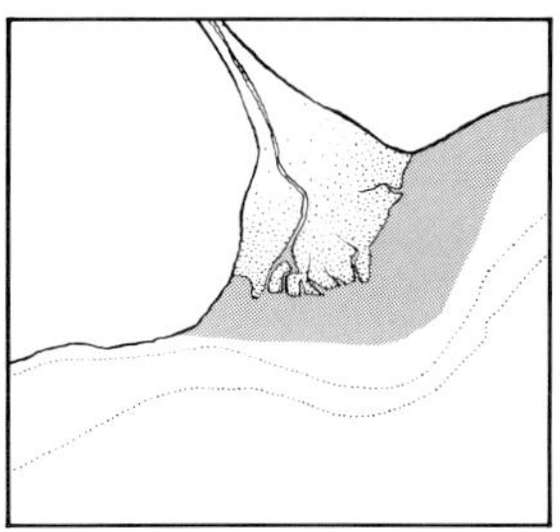

River delta
Lyre River
Strait of Juan de Fuca,
high energy environment

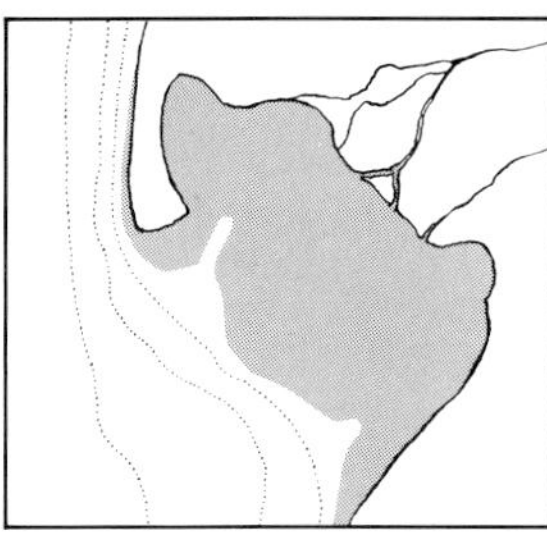

Tidal flats
Triangle Cove,
Camano Island

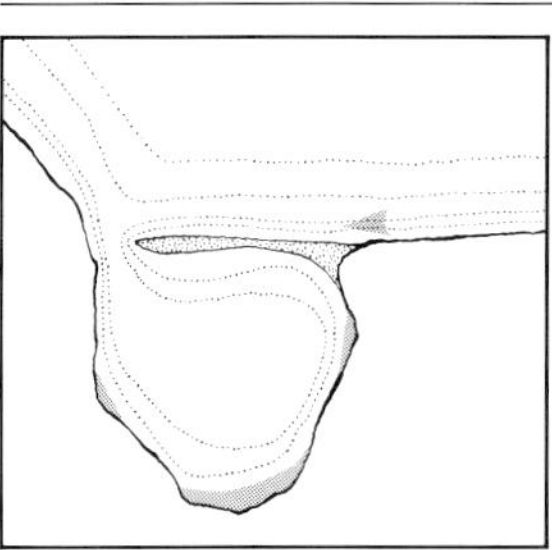

Spits
Across Vaughn Bay,
Pierce County

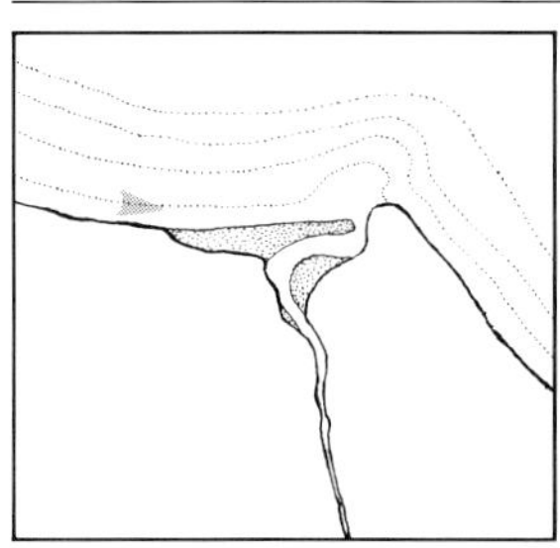

Spit deflecting the
Hoko River,
Clallam County

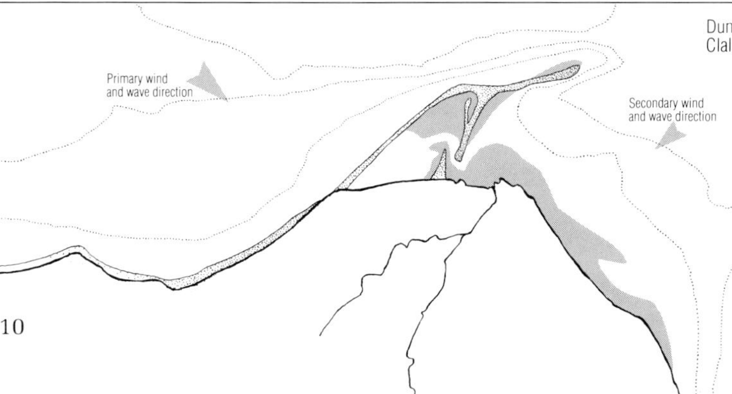

Dungeness Spit,
Clallam County

Coastal Deposition

Extensive sedimentary deposits form in coastal areas where the supply of sediment exceeds its removal by waves. The largest deposits in Puget Sound formed under this condition are river deltas, but tidal flats, salt marshes, spits, tombolos, cuspate forelands, and dunes result from them as well. The appearance and relative location of major features in the coastal zone are illustrated in Figures 1.8 and 1.9.

River deltas form where a stream or river discharges sediment to an estuary or coastal area faster than it is removed by marine processes. Deltas of many sizes occur in Puget Sound.

Tidal flats develop in partially enclosed or protected waters where there is low wave energy and a supply of sediment from tidal currents or a nearby river. In the past 5,000 years, tidal mud flats in Puget Sound have formed at the mouths of most rivers and at the heads of quiet bays. They have a complex pattern of branching channels through which water and sediment are moved with the tides.

A spit is a narrow ridge of sand and gravel, exposed at high water, that extends from shore into deep water. The sand and gravel supplied by coastal erosion is transported to the spit by nearshore currents, and deposited where these currents slow in deep water or are diverted by a change in the alignment of the coast.

Spits may be relatively straight where waves come from one direction such as the spit across Vaughn Bay in Pierce County and the one west of Steamboat Island. More commonly, waves coming from a secondary direction and wave refraction and diffraction will produce an inward curve at the offshore ends of spits. A recurved spit can be seen at Dungeness.

Spits tend to straighten the coastline with time. They grow across indentations in the shore and deflect mouths of streams and rivers in the direction of longshore transport, such as at Kydaka Point. Spits have even formed across major bays, such as Sequim Bay, where the longshore transport directions vary seasonally and multiple spits have formed at the bay mouth.

On exposed shores with adequate sediment supply and where wind and wave patterns are complex, very large spits form with intricate shapes. Dungeness Spit, in the Strait of Juan de Fuca, is one of the largest features of this type in the world. Ediz Hook is another example nearby. The dominant wind and wave direction is from the west where sand, supplied by cliff erosion, is carried alongshore and deposited at the offshore end of these spits. At Dungeness, strong northeasterly winds occur diurnally (daily) in the summer and during winter storms. These winds cause a reversal of longshore transport at the outer end of Dungeness Spit where Graveyard Spit has developed from this secondary supply of sediment.

Figure 1.9 Coastal features formed by sediment deposition—dunes, forelands, and tombolos.

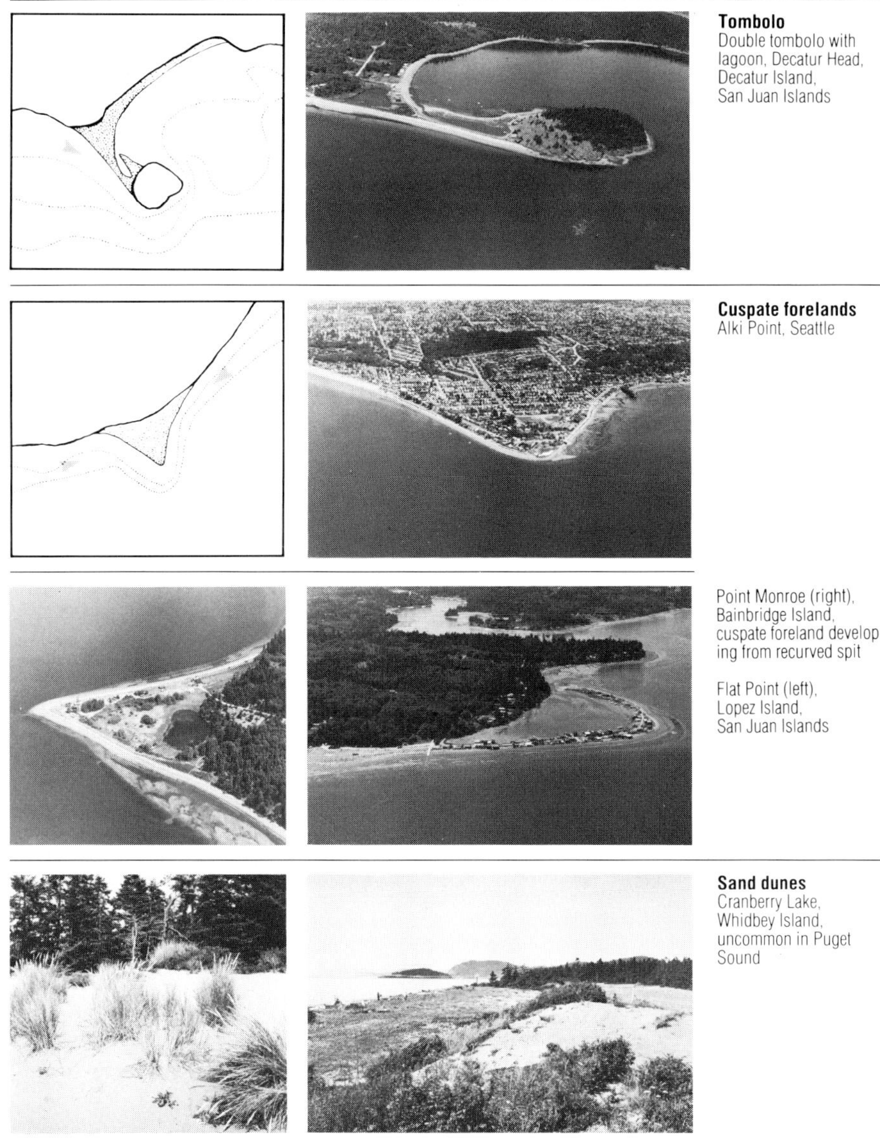

A tombolo is a spit that connects an island with the adjacent shore. The sediments comprising a tombolo may come from two sources: beach sand from the mainland, and material eroded by waves from the island itself. Tombolos form in the wave shadow, or lee side, of the island where the shore is protected from large waves. They have a variety of shapes depending on the dimensions of the island, its distance from shore, and the way in which sediment is supplied. A single tombolo is one in which a single sandbar connects the island to the mainland. A double tombolo has two sandbars extending to the shore from the island, enclosing a shallow lagoon. Double tombolos usually form in areas with seasonal shifts in the direction of longshore transport.

Cuspate forelands are large triangular or cusp-like sedimentary deposits along the shore. Cuspate forelands in Puget Sound vary from hundreds of meters to kilometers in length. They may be formed by:

- converging wave directions occurring in the lee of offshore shoals—analogous to a tombolo except that a submarine feature rather than an island exists offshore;
- seasonal changes in longshore transport directions inside a bay that produce a triangular deposit of sand where currents meet;
- recurved spits that connect with the shore at both ends, enclosing a lagoon that fills with sediment and becomes a marsh.

Sand dunes are wind-formed deposits. The sand comprising coastal sand dunes comes from adjacent beaches. Dunes normally occur near beaches with wide backshores where there is abundant sand and strong wind. They are rare in Puget Sound though examples occur near Cranberry Lake on northwest Whidbey Island.

Coastal Erosion

Some parts of the coastal zone are characterized by high sandy cliffs or steep slopes of resistant bedrock that plunge to the beach or directly into water. In these areas, tidal fluctuations allow waves to strike directly on the sea cliffs, eroding the coastal rocks and sediments. Coastal erosion would appear to be a simple mechanical result of waves impacting rock. Actually, several processes contribute to the removal of material from coastal cliffs. These include:

- quarrying—extraction of rocks or sedimentary material by air and water pressures in breaking waves;
- abrasion—grinding of coastal rocks by wave-agitated sand and gravel;
- water layer weathering—rock disintegration by chemical reactions with sea water and salt crystallization pressures;
- biological—burrowing and scraping of coastal rock by organisms, and dissolution caused by biological activity.

As cliffs erode, the loose material falls onto the beach where it is sorted by size and varying amounts are removed by waves and currents. The beaches in areas undergoing erosion reflect an imbalance between the supply of material from the adjacent cliff and its removal by waves. If the supply of sediment is large relative to the transporting capabilities of the waves and nearshore currents, then an extensive backshore

Figure 1.10 Coastal features produced by erosion. Quarrying and abrasion over the past several thousand years have produced sea cliffs and stacks of bedrock along exposed rocky shores. Cobble-armored beaches (bottom photo) form where sand is eroded by waves.

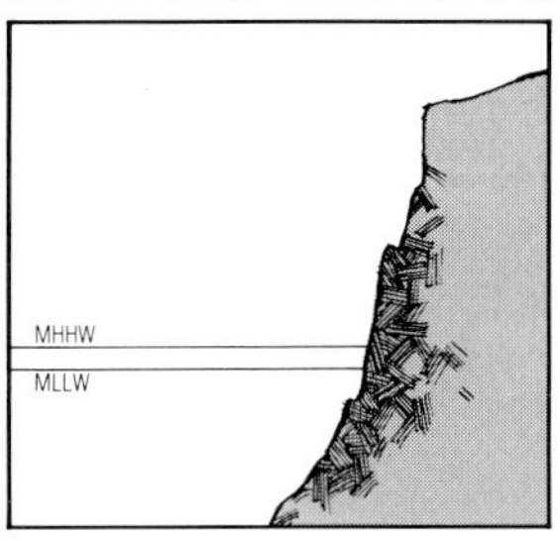

Sea cliffs
Turn Point,
Stuart Island,
San Juan Islands

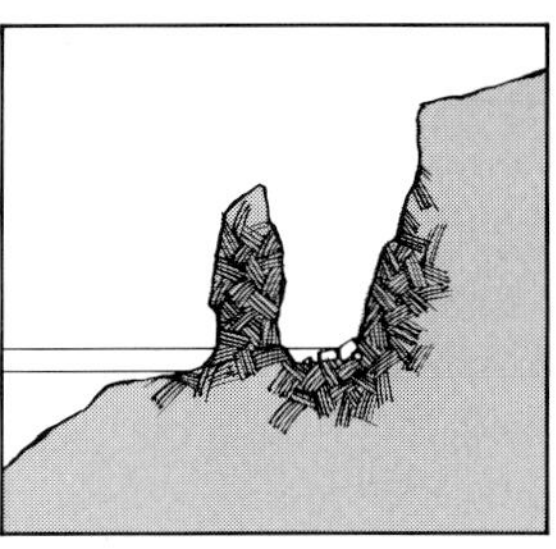

Sea stack
Near Neah Bay,
Strait of Juan de Fuca

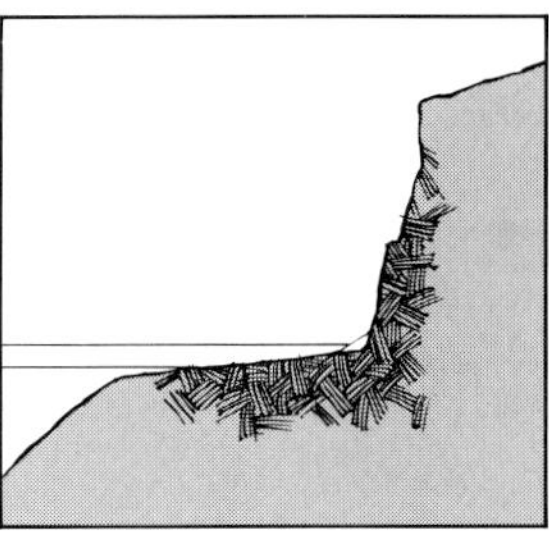

Wave cut platforms
Formed by erosion of bedrock, Sucia Island, San Juan Islands

Formed by erosion of glacial till, Redondo Beach, King County

area develops (Fig. 1.5). At the other extreme, when the sediment supply is limited, large waves and strong currents may remove the sand and mud from a beach and leave behind the gravel, cobbles, and boulders that are too large to be transported. The resulting layer of coarse sediments is called a residual deposit, and its effect is to armor the beach face, protecting it from further erosion. Removal of this protective layer for any purpose may begin a new cycle of beach erosion accompanied by a loss of beach and perhaps a retreating coastline.

Coastal erosion produces a variety of features that affect conditions on adjacent beaches. Some of these features characteristic of coasts around Puget Sound are illustrated in Figure 1.10. The shore platform can take on many forms depending on the geological characteristics of the cliff. Features such as fractures, bedding planes, differences in rock resistance to erosion, and mechanical strength all influence the actual shape of the shore platform. Excellent examples of the influence of rock characteristics on marine erosion are seen at the entrance to Fossil Bay on Sucia Island in San Juan County and where the Blakely Formation outcrops in central Puget Sound. Here the sedimentary beds are tilted vertically, trend in an east–west direction, and outcrop at Restoration Point near Port Blakely and across Puget Sound, at the Alki Point lighthouse. Waves have selectively eroded the less resistant beds on the shore platform, producing a crenulated surface rather than a smooth one as is common along shores cut into glacial material.

Where the wave energy is high and/or the cliff materials are very susceptible to erosion, sea cliffs can retreat substantial distances under the attack of waves. The cliff at the west side of Smith Island, for example, erodes at the average rate of 0.69 meters (2.3 feet) per year. In other areas sea cliff instability is related more to upland geology than to wave activity, as in Seattle at Discovery Park on the south side of West Point and in the Magnolia Bluff area, where landslides have occurred.

Figure 2.1 Monthly runoff of the Deschutes and Snohomish rivers. Snow accumulation in the Snohomish watershed results in a winter minimum. Deschutes River runoff coincides with precipitation because its watershed does not receive much snow.

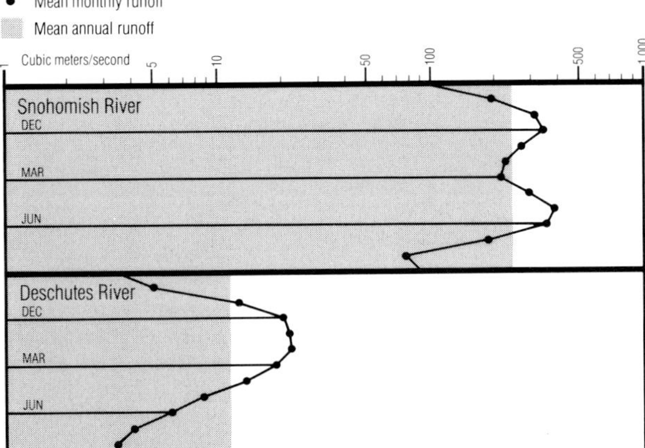

Figure 2.2 Circulation and paths of sediment transport near a river mouth. Onshore flow at the bottom (solid arrows) traps sediment near the river mouth.

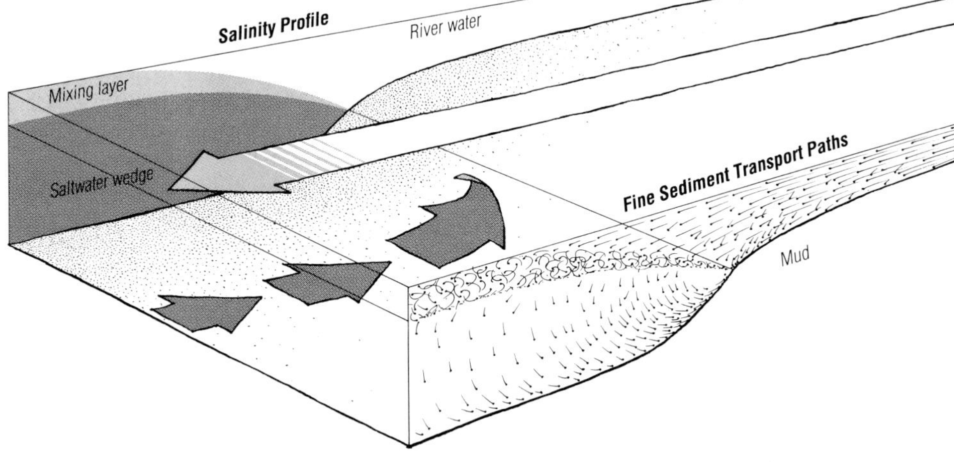

Figure 2.3 Tidal mud flat and a small delta in Oakland Bay, Mason County.

CHAPTER 2

River Deltas

Rivers and streams rate well below the glaciers as suppliers of sediments for building coastal landforms in Puget Sound, and yet their imprints on shore evolution in the region have been major. The most remarkable features are the large deltas that have formed at the mouths of major river valleys since the last glaciation. These deltas developed where the rivers delivered a sufficiently large supply of sediment to fill up their lower valleys as the sea rose to its present level. Major river deltas have advanced substantial distances into the deep basins of Puget Sound, creating large areas of alluvium. These lands are agriculturally rich and also highly valued for industrial and commercial uses.

The currents and patterns of sedimentation at river mouths which give rise to these alluvial deposits are here described in general terms. In addition, several of the major river deltas are discussed in greater detail because of their unique geologic history or relevance to development of the coastal zone.

Currents and Sediments Near Rivers

Delta growth has a seasonal nature that is linked to the variation of freshwater discharge during the year. This variation is illustrated in Figure 2.1 which shows the mean monthly discharge of the Snohomish and Deschutes rivers for a 30-year period. Similar variation in discharge occurs during the year in most of the larger rivers that receive both rainwater and snowmelt from the mountains. The relative height of the winter and spring discharge peaks varies from river to river depending on the proportion of the drainage area that is covered with snow. Rivers draining mountainous areas have peak discharges during the spring thaw, whereas those draining exclusively lowland areas have peak flows during the rainy periods of late fall and early winter.

Fresh water discharged from rivers and streams drives a system of currents which moves the sediment that forms deltas at river mouths. In sheltered bays where waves and tidal currents do not mix the fresh runoff with the underlying denser salt water, stratification of the water column develops and a slow landward flow of salt water near the bottom occurs (Fig. 2.2). This circulation pattern provides a return path for fine sediment as it settles out of the river plume. Fine sediment is trapped near river mouths in this manner and forms the mud shoals and tidal flats that exist at the heads of most protected bays (Fig. 2.3). Sediment deposition rates can be very high in these areas and are a critical factor to be considered in the design of port facilities and navigation channels because costly maintenance dredging may be necessary.

During periods of high discharge, currents are sufficiently strong to transport sand and gravel on the deltas. Transport rates of sand and gravel are particularly high at the lower stages of the tide. At these times freshwater flow is largely restricted to the distributary channels and is in contact with the channel bed. During high tide the fast freshwater current is displaced from the channels by a wedge of denser salt water and very little material is transported along the channel beds.

Wetlands Accretion

The seaward progression of the shoreline across the delta with time creates new wetlands by a process requiring joint contributions by biological and physical agents. A large fraction of alluvial soil is fine-grained mineral material transported to the river delta by flood waters and tidal currents. In order for this material to settle out of suspension, current speeds must be very low, usually less than 0.20 meters per second (0.4 knots). Tidal flows infiltrate the wetlands through a network of small channels and disperse suspended sediment among the marsh vegetation. Marshes are also inundated during winter and spring floods when sediment-laden river water overflows the distributary channel levees. Once sediment-laden waters flood the marshes, resistance of the vegetation slows the water, and fine sediment can then settle out among the plants. Since the current speed required to resuspend it is much greater than the current speed when deposition occurred, it is trapped there and the soil level builds upward as additional fine mineral material is added. Figure 2.4 shows sediment mounds in salt marsh vegetation that have developed by this process.

Marsh Plants

A very special plant community has adapted to the frequent shifting of the sand and gravel substrate by wind and waves and to the wide fluctuations in the salinity near the delta shore. The outer perimeter beach is the main line of defense that protects unconsolidated deposits in the wetlands from wave attack. At high tide most of the wave energy that reaches the delta is dissipated there. Just landward of the berm the substrate remains relatively undisturbed for periods of a year or more between major storms. Small isolated plant communities spring up in bunches among the drift logs and other beach debris. Yellow abronia, silver beachweed, European beachgrass, and American beachgrass are members of the pioneer beach plant assemblage commonly found in

Figure 2.4 Mud deposits among salt marsh vegetation, an example of geological and biological processes building wetlands together.

Figure 2.5 Beach grass, morning glory, knotweed and other shore vegetation help to stabilize berms and backshore areas and protect them from waves and wind.

Puget Sound. These stout plants provide sheltered environments that trap windblown sand which over the years builds up a beach ridge that may reach a few meters above mean higher high water (Fig. 2.5).

On top of and behind the beach ridge the mound-building plants merge into denser vegetation that tolerates windblown sand but not extensive erosion of the substrate. This community includes seashore bluegrass, large-headed sedge, gray beach pea, beach morning glory, beach knotweed, American beachgrass, American sea rocket, and beach pea. The ground cover of these plants, if dense and uniform, protects the beach ridge from wind erosion quite well. Plant roots intermesh in the sand and gravel and form a tight matrix that binds material together and anchors it to the beach ridge. The stems and foliage shelter the ridge surface from the direct attack by wind. Beach ridges built up in this manner have been augmented by man-made levees on most large river deltas.

The Major Contributors

The twelve largest rivers in the Puget lowland (not including the Fraser River) discharge about 3.2 million metric tons (3.5 million short tons) of sediment into the Puget Sound annually. The approximate volume of this sediment is 1.8 million cubic meters (2.4 million cubic yards) and were it all to be deposited on the bottom of Puget Sound (this could never happen) the estuary present today would be filled in about 83,000 years. On the average, 90 percent of a river's sediment load is suspended fine-grained material; the rest is coarser bedload, mostly sand.

Figure 2.6 illustrates the runoff and sediment discharge of major rivers in the Puget lowland. Mean annual and average monthly runoff values are based on river gauging over the 30-year period from 1931 to 1960 and accurately represent the hydrology of these rivers. The sediment discharge data, however, were acquired during 1- to 2-year periods between 1964 and 1966 and are useful only for comparing sediment loads on a relative basis. It is not known if sediment loads during these years were representative of the long-term averages for any of these rivers.

The five rivers in the northern half of the Puget lowland, the Elwha, Nooksack, Skagit, Stillaguamish, and Snohomish, contribute 70 percent of the fresh water discharged into Washington's intracoastal waters. Four of these rivers, the Nooksack, Skagit, Stillaguamish, and Snohomish, introduce more than 69 percent of the fluvial sediment to the same area. It is not surprising, therefore, that the largest deltas are located in the northern lowland. The group of rivers including the Nooksack, Dungeness, Elwha, Skagit, Snohomish, Puyallup, and Nisqually has a similar annual cycle of runoff. Early fall runoff is low following the dry summer months; sediment discharge is at a minimum at this time as well. Runoff and sediment loads increase to a maximum during the early winter months when there are frequent storms. The heavy precipitation from winter storms falls on ground unprotected by snow at the lower elevations so that soil erosion produces large suspended loads in these rivers. During this period, flooding of bottomlands occurs and high velocity currents move sediment, accumulated in the river channels during lower water stages, onto the delta platform.

As the pattern of monthly runoff suggests, the deltas of these rivers receive a large fraction of their annual sediment input in early winter and late spring. A dip in runoff follows the winter peak because much of the precipitation is stored temporarily in the snow pack of the high catchment basins. High precipitation continues during the spring and rising air temperatures in the mountains melt the snow pack, releasing large volumes of meltwater to the drainage system. The combined runoff from meltwater and seasonally high precipitation produces a spring

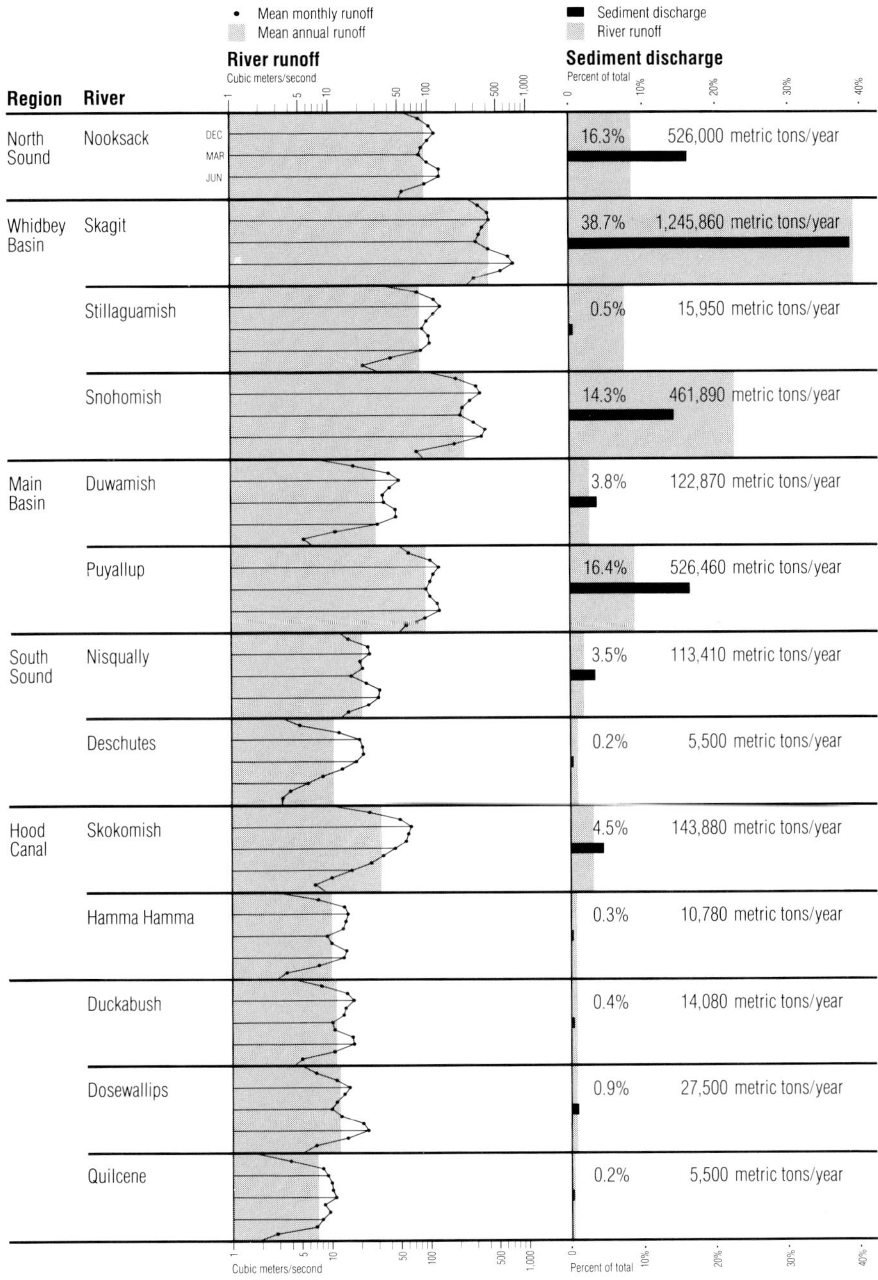

Figure 2.6 River runoff (left) and sediment discharge (right) of major rivers in Puget Sound. Proportions of total sediment discharge (3.22 metric tons/year) contributed by individual rivers is indicated by percentages. Note that the sediment loads of the Puyallup and Nooksack rivers are large in proportion to runoff but the Stillaguamish and Snohomish rivers are relatively clear.

peak that is higher than the winter peak in most years. Suspended loads in rivers during spring floods are not as large as one would expect from the high runoff since the ground is protected from the direct impact of rain by a layer of snow and soil erosion at higher elevations is less severe.

The watersheds of the Green and Deschutes rivers are at low elevations and very little precipitation is stored in a snow pack during the rainy winter months. Consequently, the runoff and sediment discharge follow the same seasonal trends as the regional precipitation. Seasonal variation in the Stillaguamish runoff is a hybrid of the two above patterns; the winter peak is larger than the spring peak. A lower yet significant proportion of the catchment basin is at high altitudes; thus the large winter maximum in precipitation predominates the runoff curve.

Pristine Deltas

The Nisqually and Nooksack deltas are the most studied examples of sedimentation at river mouths in Puget Sound. In comparison with other large deltas in the region, only minor aspects of them have been modified by man, so they provide good examples of natural sedimentary features.

Nisqually delta Figure 2.7 illustrates the major parts of the Nisqually in cross section. The inner delta extends landward of mean higher high water and consists of low-lying wetlands dissected by many shallow tidal and distributary channels. The freshwater discharge and sediment load of the river pass through a network of distributary channels on route to the Sound. Between these distributaries small marshy islands form. The outer delta is intertidal and lacks the terrestrial marsh vegetation of the inner delta. Like the inner delta, the intertidal surface is flat and is divided by a complex pattern of tidal channels. At the outer edge, the slope of the delta front steepens and dips offshore into deeper water. The horizontal sedimentary beds that make up the delta platform are called topset beds. These consist of mud deposits rich in organic material that accumulate in the inner delta wetlands, sand deposits in tidal and distributary channels, and other intertidal sediments of finer texture. The delta front consists of steeper foreset beds which have accreted seaward over the previously existing bottom sediment. Foreset and bottomset beds usually consist of mud and fine sand. As the delta front advances out into deeper water with time, more and more sediment is required to produce new surface area on the delta platform. Therefore the rate of seaward advance of the shoreline as the delta grows in volume will decline with a constant supply of river sediment.

The river is the major supplier of sediments to the Nisqually delta. It discharges about 0.11 million metric tons (0.12 million short tons) of material into Nisqually Reach annually and ranks fourth as a sediment source among the major rivers. The sand and fine material carried by the river move through the inner delta wetlands in the large distributaries. Because the sediment transport is confined to channels, very little of it accumulates on the inner delta. When the river's sediment load reaches the intertidal delta, the sediment dispersal pattern is determined by the height of the tide and the intensity of wave and current activity at the distributary mouths. At low tide the suspended load and bedload are transported across the intertidal delta in shallow channels that are extensions of the main distributaries. At high tide these channels are submerged and the plume of suspended sediment is moved about by tidal and nearshore currents, and the transport of sand and coarser material on the bed ceases. Longshore transport is another process that carries sediment to the Nisqually delta. Compared with the river sediment load, the longshore contributions of sediment are of minor importance, but they are vital to the stability of the beaches on other more exposed deltas. Longshore transport provides the coarse material to form berms and beach ridges that can protect the marshes and wetlands from wave attack.

Sediment from the Nisqually River and longshore sources can leave the delta along the coast or across the delta front. Some of the material transported along the shore remains in the nearshore zone and is incorporated directly into the delta transport system. Bedload material, primarily sand from the river, however, follows a more complex route before it leaves the delta. At high tide, the bedload accumulates in bars or shoals near the distributary mouths. These bars are eroded by the river when it reoccupies distributary channels on the falling tide. Some of this material is dispersed on the intertidal platform by waves and tidal currents; the rest is transported in the distributary channels to the delta front. Some of the sand dispersed from the distributary channels is moved onshore by waves and accumulates on the beach. This sand then becomes part of the beach and moves along the delta shoreline and down the coast.

The suspended load of the Nisqually River can escape the delta via more direct routes. At low tide it is injected into the tidal flow at the delta front as a muddy plume which is dispersed from the delta during subsequent tidal cycles. During higher tidal phases the plume of suspended material disperses across the intertidal delta because the denser saline water displaces the fresh water above its channel bed. Part of the material settles to the bed by the process illustrated in Figure 2.2; the rest is carried offshore by the falling tide. Because of its moderate wave climate, the Nisqually delta is an excellent example of deltaic sedimentation controlled almost entirely by tidal and fluvial currents.

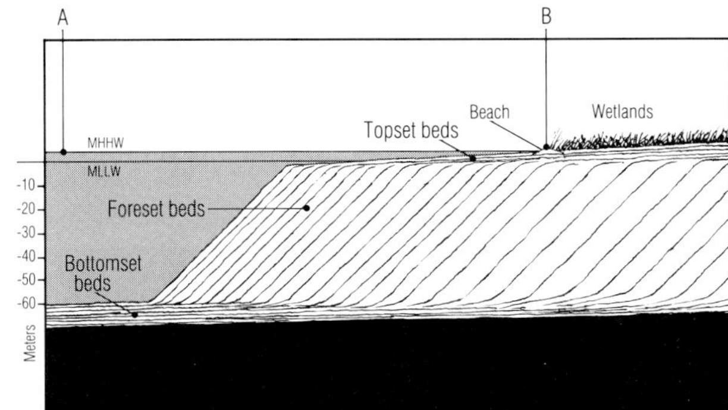

Figure 2.7 Simplified cross section of the Nisqually delta illustrating its major parts. Points A and B are located on Figure 2.8.

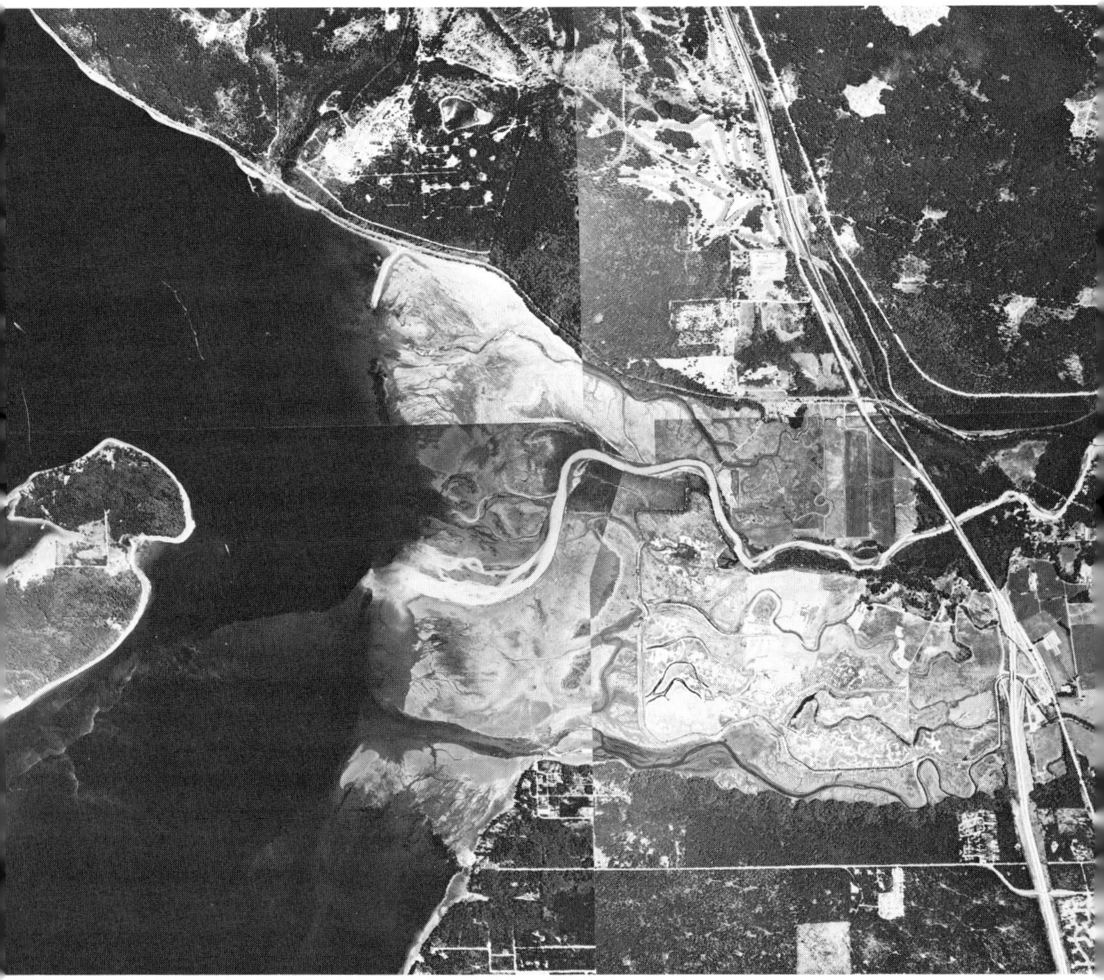

Photo mosaic of the Nisqually delta at low tide. The main distributary appears white because of the glacial rock flour suspended in the river. (Photo courtesy Corps of Engineers.)

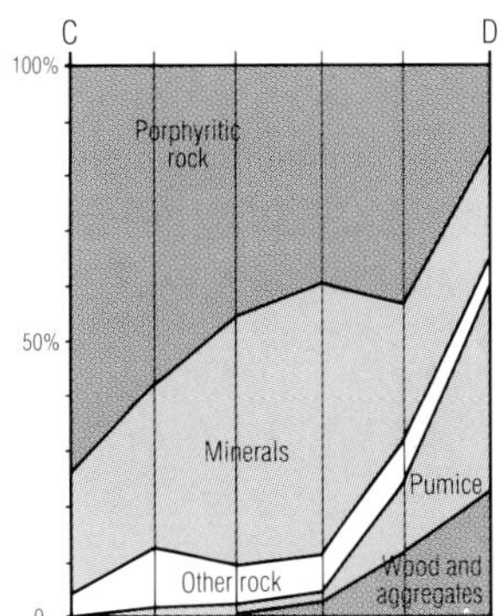

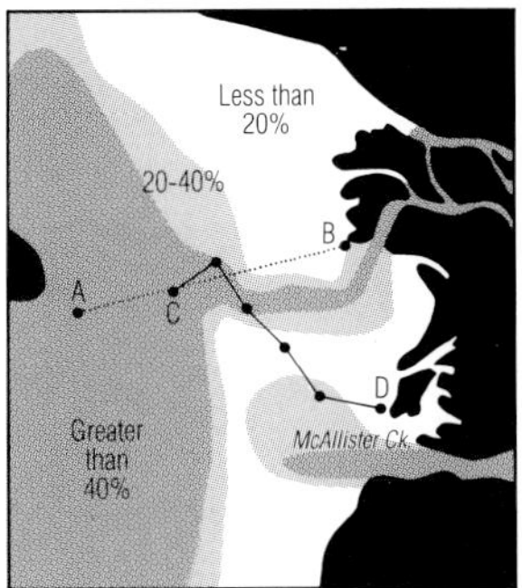

Figure 2.8 Distribution and composition of sand in Niqually delta sediments.

Since the last glaciation, the Nisqually has filled an inlet with sediment and advanced into the basin at about 50 meters (160 feet) per century. The constriction of the channel connecting the south and central basins of Puget Sound by delta sediment increased the tidal current speeds there until an equilibrium between sediment deposition and dispersal by currents was eventually reached. During the final phase of delta formation, these strong tidal flows carried most of the sediment away from the center of the delta. More extensive outward growth occurred along the east and west margins where tidal flows were weaker. The unique crescent shape of the outer Nisqually delta reflects these final events in its development.

The processes that move river sediment through the nearshore environment are evident in composition, particle size, and distribution of sediments on the delta surface. Before dams were built on the Nisqually River, much of the bedload carried to the delta derived from volcanic rocks exposed at the river's source near Mt. Rainier. Evidence of a volcanic origin is quite apparent in the intertidal and marsh sediments where a large portion of the coarse material consists of volcanic rock fragments. This dense material resists erosion and forms deposits on the outer delta where tidal currents are vigorous. Pumice, a low-density volcanic material, is abundant in the silty sediments on the tidal flats near shore where currents are weak. Figure 2.8 illustrates the variation in abundance of these and other sediments across the delta.

Sand is abundant in the main distributary, on the delta front, and in the tidal channel at the mouth of McAllister Creek (Fig. 2.8). The high percentage of sand in these deposits indicates that the sediments in these areas are moved primarily as bedload. As the tidal and distributary channels meander across the intertidal delta, they spread some of their sand load in finger-like deposits that extend out from the shoreline. The tidal flats to the east and west of the main distributary are covered with finer material that contains up to 90 percent silt. Silt deposition occurs during river floods and high tides when there is little

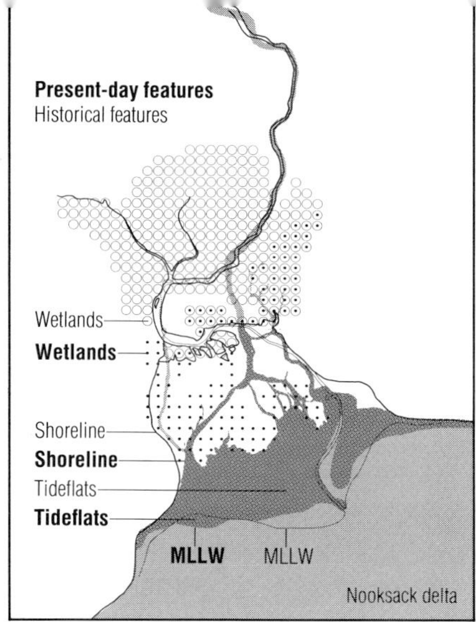

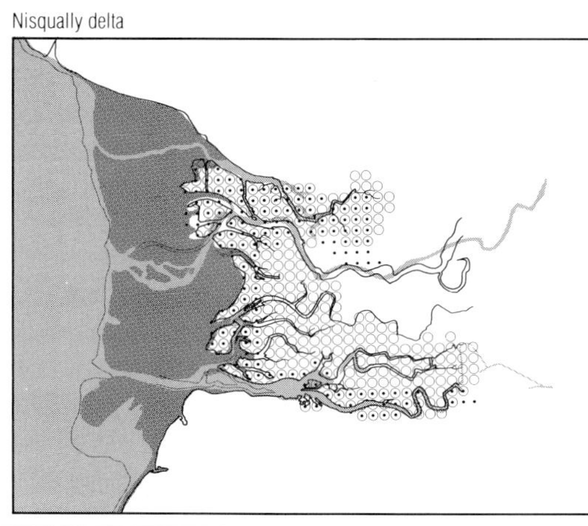

Figure 2.9 Physical changes on the Nooksack and Nisqually deltas during the past century. Extensive new wetlands have formed on the Nooksack delta; whereas the Nisqually delta has retreated slightly. (Source: Bortleson et al., 1979)

wave activity. Some sand is resuspended by storm waves and is carried away from the channels; small quantities of sand transported in this way are intermixed with the silts on the tidal flats.

Winter and late spring floods are vital to the Nisqually wetlands because they supply the marshes with the fine sediment necessary for continued growth. Although the shoreline at the mouth of the Nisqually has been quite stable since 1878, Figure 2.9 shows that small losses of wetlands area, about 1.6 square kilometers (0.62 square miles), have occurred around the marshy islands near the main distributary. These losses may have resulted from natural shifts in the channel location that have occurred in the past 100 years.

More pronounced changes have occurred at the delta front since 1878. The intertidal delta has retreated 75 to 300 meters (250–1,000 feet) and it appears that the rate of sediment supply to the delta front is not in balance with the rate of removal by tidal currents. Although the cause of the imbalance is not known with certainty, a reduction in the supply of fluvial sediment is the most plausible explanation.

Nooksack delta This delta has undergone the most dramatic growth of any coastal sedimentary feature in the Puget Sound region in recent times. Its growth is a good example of an imbalance between marine processes, waves, and nearshore currents that remove sediment from the delta and the supply of river sediment to the delta. Wetlands have advanced seaward over 1.5 kilometers (0.93 miles) on the intertidal platform, producing 3.0 square kilometers (1.16 square miles) of new bottomland. The area of the intertidal delta has decreased as portions of it have evolved into subaerial wetlands. The eastern corner, however, is encroaching on Bellingham Bay, creating costly shoaling problems in some navigation channels. These historical trends in the development of the Nooksack delta are illustrated in Figure 2.9. Between 1888 and 1972, the main river channel has cut across a large oxbow. Several small interdistributary islands at the former river mouth have coalesced into a much larger one, occupying the western half of the river valley, and islands have formed in the eastern half of the valley as well. Just west of Marrietta, longshore movement of sand from the river has formed a spit 0.3 kilometers (0.19 miles) long that is growing across the mouth of the east distributary channel. What was an intertidal bay fewer than 100 years ago now is a group of islands that has extended the coastline out to the mouth of the river valley.

The intertidal platform of the Nooksack delta is covered with a layer of medium sand that contains about 12 percent silt and clay. Numerous shallow distributary channels 1.2 to 1.5 meters (4–5 feet) deep have cut across the delta platform sand. At low tide the bedload from the river moves seaward in these channels, but during high tide wave and tidal currents disperse the channel sands evenly over the delta platform. The two-step process by which river sand is distributed over the intertidal delta is probably not continuous, rather it requires storms to produce wind waves large enough to move the sand away from the channels. Small waves during calm weather move these sands only in the breaker zone. Part of the river-derived sand on the inner delta is transported onshore by waves and nourishes the beaches along the seaward shores of the interdistributary islands. Continued growth of these beaches with new material from the delta platform is important to the growth of the wetlands here.

Very little river silt and clay are deposited permanently on the intertidal delta. Waves and tidal currents are sufficiently vigorous to keep this material in suspension and carry it to the deeper water seaward of the delta front. Deposits of this material 1.5 to 6.1 meters (4.9–20 feet) thick have accumulated in the northern half of Bellingham Bay in postglacial time.

Developed Deltas

Duwamish delta The Duwamish delta is the best example in the Puget Sound region of a natural delta completely altered by man. Without historical survey data, it is nearly impossible to recognize any of the delta's natural features. Prior to channel straightening, the Duwamish River meandered widely over a sinuous course on the flood plain now the site of Boeing Field and the south Seattle industrial com-

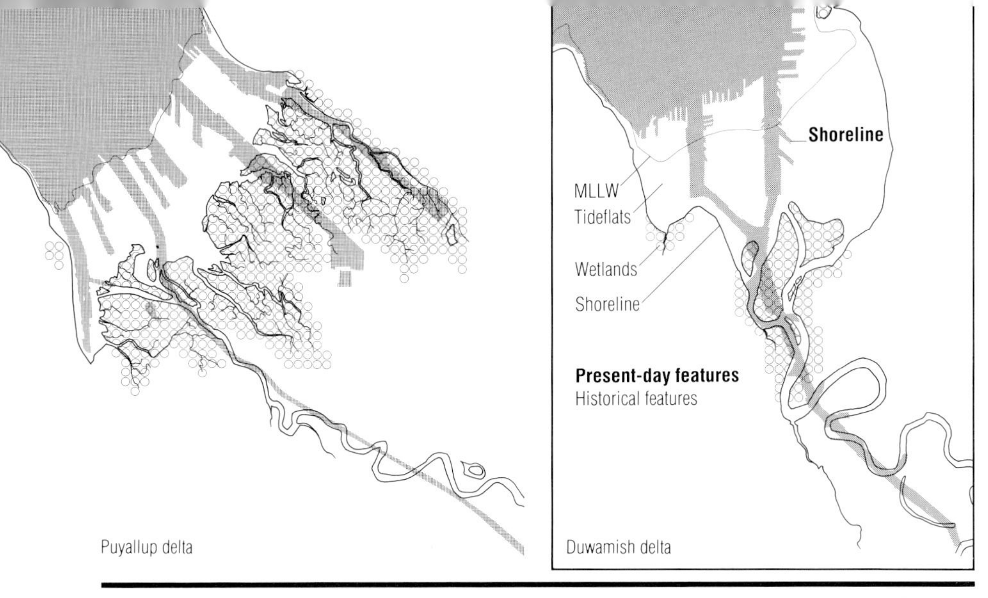

Figure 2.10 Deltas like the Puyallup and Duwamish in urban and industrial areas have been altered drastically by man. Former river channels, wetlands, and intertidal areas are no longer recognizable. (Source: Bortleson et al., 1979)

plex (Fig. 2.10). Two small inlets, remnants of old river meanders, still exist in the Georgetown district of Seattle. In 1854, the river flowed into Elliott Bay through a group of four interdistributary islands. These wetlands and nearly all of the intertidal delta platform have been filled and developed by the City of Seattle, representing a loss of about 10.8 square kilometers (4.2 square miles). Although few would dispute the long-term benefits of this commitment of resources, there remain certain costs to be paid for these benefits. Ground instability of hydraulically filled areas and degraded water quality are but two examples. Subsidence along the Duwamish waterway occurred during the 1949 and 1965 earthquakes and other ground failures have occurred more recently on areas improperly and unsafely filled.

Puyallup delta Like the former Duwamish delta, the natural Puyallup delta (Fig. 2.10) is now unrecognizable as a result of extensive man-made alterations. The Port of Tacoma has extended large piers across the intertidal platform to the delta front and across the width of Commencement Bay's southeast shore. The Hylebos, Port Industrial, and Puyallup waterways have been dredged through former wetlands. A total commitment of 17.3 square kilometers (6.7 square miles) of delta surface was made in the past century to develop Tacoma's port and industrial facilities of which 10 square kilometers (6.1 square miles) were formerly wetlands.

The Puyallup River rates second jointly with the Nooksack as a sediment source in the Puget lowland where it discharges 0.5 million

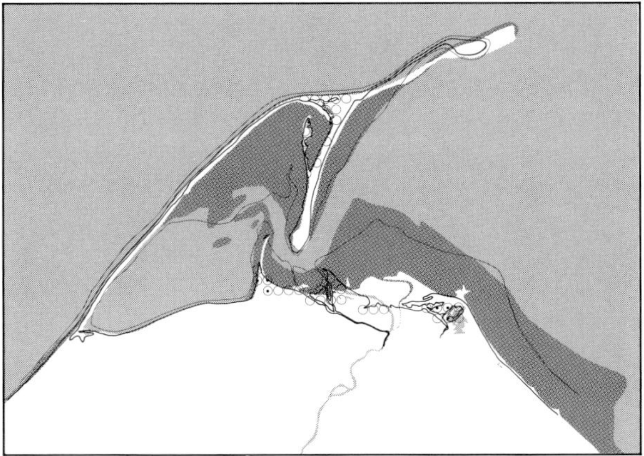

Figure 2.11 New tideflats and wetlands have formed on the Dungeness delta, and Dungeness Spit has grown over the past century. The spit has grown 500 meters since 1855. (Source: Bortleson et al., 1979)

metric tons (0.6 short tons) of sediment into Commencement Bay annually. Commencement Bay is an ideal location for a port in many respects because the bay is sheltered from direct wave attack and it is near large population and industrial centers. Since it was once a natural delta system, however, sedimentation is a major problem in the artificially deepened navigation channels and waterways. Tidal currents in the bay are weak, causing much of the river's sediment load to accumulate in the navigation channels where it must be removed by dredging. The annual cost of channel maintenance offsets some of the cost benefits arising from the port facilities' geographical location.

High Energy Deltas

Dungeness delta The Dungeness River ranks last both in terms of mean annual runoff and estimated sediment discharge (90 metric tons [100 short tons] per year). Nonetheless, the recent history of sedimentation on its delta has been an eventful one. The 1855 survey of the delta revealed that a complex of spits had formed east of the present-day river mouth. These spits have grown across the delta front in a westerly direction substantially increasing the wetlands at the river mouth (Fig. 2.11). The river mouth shifted about 600 meters (1,970 feet) to the east during the same period and eroded a small spit in the process. Duck Spit has extended at the rate of about 5 meters (16 feet) per year into Dungeness Bay. The outer edge of the intertidal platform is now located up to 0.50 kilometers (0.31 miles) farther offshore than in 1855.

These recent depositional events indicate that the fluvial sediment input to the delta has exceeded the rate of sediment removal by dispersal processes. Waves and tidal currents, nevertheless, have caused significant redistribution of fluvial sediment on the delta, and the shape of the intertidal and wetlands areas near the river mouth shows signs of substantial reworking. For example, tidal currents have cut an S-shaped channel across the western portion of the tidal flats. This channel is maintained by the scouring action of water flow in and out of Dungeness Bay. Wind waves approaching from the northeast have built a spit that deflects the main distributary about 0.40 kilometers (1,300 feet) to the west. The future of the Dungeness delta depends critically on the continued existence of Dungeness Spit as a natural wave barrier. The spit has grown steadily over the past 120 years at the rate of 4.5 meters (15 feet) per year and, unlike Ediz Hook, it appears to be a very stable feature. Consequently, continued seaward growth of the Dungeness delta is expected.

Elwha delta The Elwha River flows into the deep and exposed waters of the Strait of Juan de Fuca. Its flood plain fills a shallow valley in the northern foothills of the Olympics. The delta is lobe-shaped, symmetrical, and lacks the interdistributary islands and extensive wetlands that fringe other deltas formed in less exposed waterways. At the present time, the Elwha River supplies very little sediment to Puget Sound. There is evidence, however, that the Elwha River was a very prominent sediment source in the recent geologic past.

Soon after the glaciers receded, the gradient of the river channel was steep, cutting across extensive deposits of unconsolidated glacial material that had formed between the Olympic foothills and the ice-blocked Strait of Juan de Fuca. The glacial material was easily eroded and the river discharged large quantities of it into the Strait, forming an extensive delta. Various stages in the growth of this delta are illustrated in Figure 2.12. The area of the ancestral delta during its early growth was at least five times that of the present one. Moreover, it appears that the prevailing direction of wave approach and longshore transport was from west to east as it is today. This is indicated by the more extensive sedimentation that occurred to the east of the river mouth and by the short east-trending spits that developed on the downdrift flank of the delta. Rising sea level and concurrent shore bluff erosion gradually shifted the location of these spits eastward and onshore. Eventually a single large spit developed at the site of Ediz Hook and evolved into the feature seen today. As sea level rose from 33 meters (108 feet) to the present level, the gradient of the river decreased and the supply of glacial sediment along its lower reaches diminished, causing a reduction in the sediment discharge to the delta. Wave activity during this period probably remained nearly constant and at some point began removing

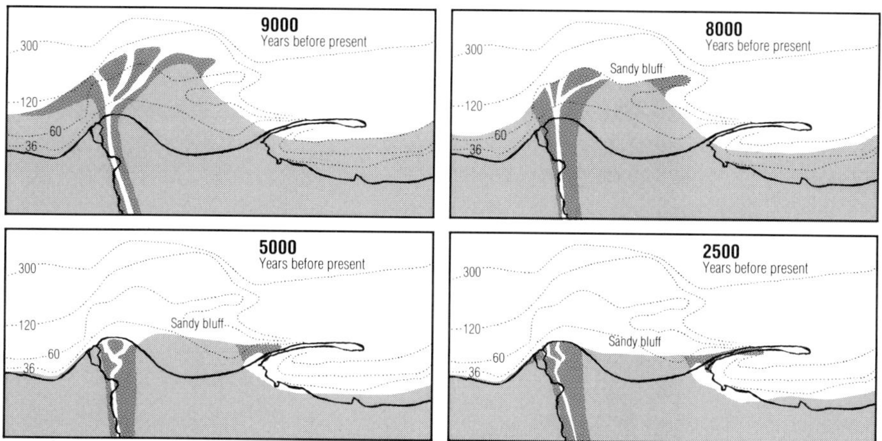

Figure 2.12 Geological history of the Elwha delta and Ediz Hook over the past 9,000 years. Rising sea level and wave erosion have diminished the delta's size and moved much of its original sediment to Ediz Hook.

fluvial sediment from the delta front at about the same rate it was discharged there. The equilibrium between sediment supply and dispersal resulted in the smaller delta that exists today. The evolution of the Elwha delta is one of the better known examples of how the interaction among changing sea level, nearshore, and fluvial processes can influence the sedimentary features along the Puget Sound coast.

The sediment budget of the Elwha delta is delicately balanced at the present time. Since 1910, the lower Elwha Dam has reduced the bedload of the Elwha River by 90 percent. The Glynes Canyon Dam, completed in 1926, has further aggravated the sediment supply problem. The current flood control procedure consists of releasing water in surges to the lower Elwha channel when the reservoir levels become critically high. These surges often occur during high water and serious flooding of the outer delta results. The procedure causes other, more permanent, damage as well. High runoff erodes the river bed and levee deposits, transporting the material to the intertidal delta. Since the supply of coarse material from the upper river is cut off by the dams, sediment is not redeposited in bottomlands between floods and the loss is a permanent one.

Accretion of wetlands on the Elwha proceeds slowly because very little sediment is supplied to the marshes. In other river systems, flooding of the interdistributary marshes occurs more frequently and less catastrophically than on the Elwha. Periodic inundation of wetlands with sediment-laden river and tidal waters provides the mineral material necessary to sustain the marsh plant community and to build up the soil profile. Tidal flooding of the Elwha delta is infrequent because of the high beach ridges that fringe the outer marshes. As a consequence of the short supply of fine-grained suspended sediment, the outer marshes have not developed above the groundwater table in many places on the delta and they are perennially swampy.

In view of the restricted sediment supply, it is surprising that the shore of the Elwha delta can survive the rigorous wave climate in the Strait of Juan de Fuca. The stability of the shore at the present time is due in part to the location of the delta at the end of the Freshwater Bay transport cell. Longshore transport of gravel and cobbles from the eroding bluffs provides continuous nourishment for the beach ridge which is the primary protection from storm wave activity. The beach ridges have a natural capacity to absorb and dissipate wave energy, due to their porosity and rough surface. Minor breaches of the beach ridge occur from time to time; and were the sediment supply from Freshwater Bay to be interrupted, major erosion problems would be experienced.

CHAPTER 3

Waves and Nearshore Currents

Waves supply energy to the beaches. They usually obtain this energy from the wind, temporarily store it as water motion (kinetic energy) and as elevated water position (potential energy) and then transmit it to the shore. Wave energy is abstract like the concept of thermal energy in the flames that heat houses or propel cars. What is more relevant here is the work done by the conversion or dissipation of the energy. Wave energy dissipated on shore performs work in many forms: driving currents; mixing nearshore waters to make them homogenous in temperature, salinity, and dissolved pollutants; washing large logs onto the beach; eroding sea cliffs; transporting sediment; and sometimes damaging man-made structures. Figure 3.1 illustrates some of the more destructive results of wave energy dissipation. Vessel wakes produce similar, but smaller scaled, effects when they break along shores of often travelled ship channels and hence are included in the following discussion.

Some Wave Basics

Waves are characterized by their height, length, and period, as shown in Figure 3.2. Wave length is the distance between successive crests, wave height is the vertical distance from the crest to the trough, and the period is the time required for two successive crests to pass a fixed point. The speed of a wave traveling along the surface is equal to the length divided by the period. The energy in a group of similar waves is proportional to the wave height squared (H^2). When there are no waves the position of the water surface is called the still water level (SWL).

With the exception of vessel wakes on a calm sea, uniform waves like the ones depicted in Figure 3.2 are rarely observed in Puget Sound. At most locations, whether or not the wind is blowing, several groups of waves with different heights, periods, and directions of travel pass one's observation point simultaneously. Combinations of wave groups (Fig. 3.3a) occur continuously at all points on a disturbed sea surface, and the random motion produced by their interaction obscures the underlying regularity of the individual waves. It is possible, however, to analyze an irregular sea statistically by making use of the notion that random wave motion at any location is actually the superposition of

Figure 3.1 Damage to structures caused by waves. Top left: Residence demolished by logs at Sandy Point, Whatcom County (Photo courtesy Tom Terich). Top right: Building on an eroding bluff at Smith Island, Strait of Juan de Fuca (Photo courtesy Tom Terich). Bottom left: Steel-reinforced concrete seawall which collapsed because of foundation erosion, Swantown, Whidbey Island. Bottom right: Washout of retaining wall and 57-inch water main west of Port Angeles, Clallam County (Photo courtesy Corps of Engineers).

many regular oscillations. In this way the motion can be separated into its component sinusoids (wave groups) and the energy or heights associated with individual wave groups estimated. Every wave group has energy related to its particular height and period. For example, a plot of energy, H^2, versus wave period or frequency could be made for the four regular wave groups of Figure 3.3a and this plot is called an energy spectrum. Wave spectra provide concise summaries of many attributes of complex wave motions.

The energy spectrum is a very practical aid to understanding the wave climate in Puget Sound as well as many engineering aspects of coastal structures affected by it. For example, one can estimate the energy in the sea surface from measured wave data. In addition, the significant wave height and period, and maximum height of the waves in a sea can be estimated from the energy spectrum. The significant wave height and period are statistical estimates of the average height and period of the highest one-third of the waves comprising the sea. In engineering work the maximum wave height is often estimated by the average of the highest one percent of the waves in the sea (H_1). H_1 is approximately 1.7 times the significant wave height. These basic con-

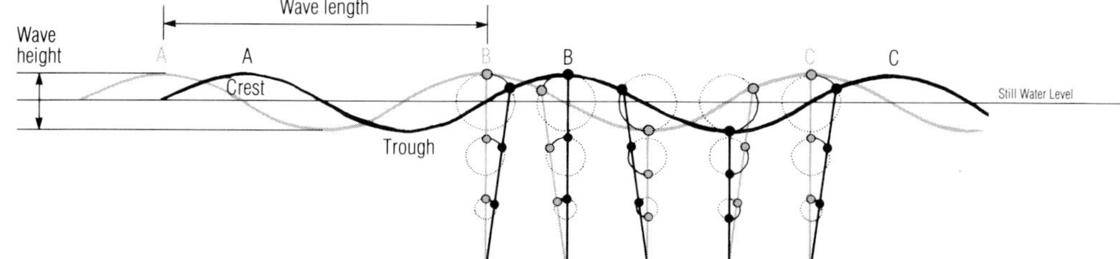

Figure 3.2 Orbital motion of water under a wave moving from right to left. Water motion is counterclockwise, from solid dots to open circles. Orbit diameters are very small at a depth equal to one half the wave length.

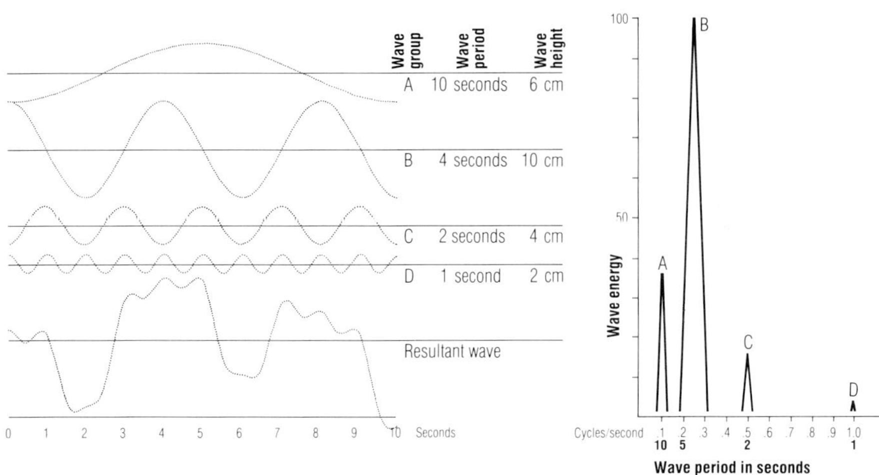

Figure 3.3 A. Left: An irregular wave (bottom) produced by the superposition of four wave groups of different heights and periods. B. Right: Energy spectrum of the resultant wave.

cepts will be discussed again in Chapter 8, which treats wave effects on coastal engineering structures in greater detail.

Generation of Waves

When a breeze begins to blow over calm water, pressure fluctuations in the moving air, and friction between it and stationary water, roughen the sea surface, generating small capillary waves.These waves are very short and unstable and break, feeding their momentum and energy to larger gravity waves as the wind speed freshens. The energy transfer from wind to sea increases rapidly during initial wave growth because the growing waves provide increased surface roughness for the wind to push against. After a short time, a truly random sea develops and the wave groups move downwind from the generation area in a broad, beamlike pattern.

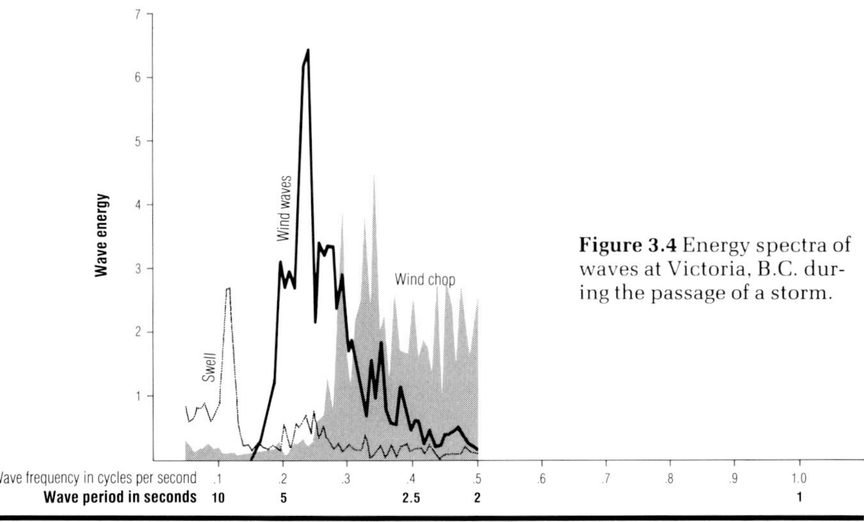

Figure 3.4 Energy spectra of waves at Victoria, B.C. during the passage of a storm.

Spectra of wave records taken during the arousal of the sea by a storm near Victoria, B.C. (Fig. 3.4) illustrate some of these events. Wave height, length, and period grow with the amount of time the wind blows and energy is transferred from the shorter waves to the longer ones. The broad and spikey appearance of the spectrum of wind chop indicates that waves with many periods are generated early in the storm. These waves create the irregular and confused appearance of the sea surface in the generation area. As the shorter waves break and dissipate, they give rise to longer ones with more uniform periods which are evident as a sharp wind wave peak in the spectrum. After the storm has gone and the sea has dissipated, only a single narrow peak remains on the spectrum. This corresponds to very regular swell waves from a distant ocean storm.

The characteristics and energy spectra of waves generated at a specific location are dependent on a variety of factors:

- average wind speed;
- amount of time the wind blows (duration);
- the shape of the water body, most significantly the length of the unobstructed surface over which the wind is blowing (fetch length) and fetch width;
- water depth;
- height of the adjacent uplands;
- preexisting sea state.

Despite the number of variables involved, it is possible to predict the spectra of waves likely to develop in an area from fetch characteristics and wind data reasonably accurately.

Except on the shallow tidal flats in the larger bays and on the major river deltas, water depth is not the main factor limiting the growth of wind waves on Puget Sound; more commonly a combination of fetch length, width, and the sheltering effects of high surrounding terrain limit their size. The ratio of fetch length to width provides a crude measure of the effect that width restriction will have on wave growth. For example, restricted fetches such as Hood Canal, Saratoga Passage, and Port Susan have length-to-width ratios ranging from 9:1 to 6:1. Even if the wind blew parallel to these fetches for a long time, the waves generated on them would have total energy and maximum wave height similar to the waves generated by the same wind on a fetch of unrestricted width, but 60 to 70 percent shorter. This ratio is of consequence in wave prediction as will become clear in Chapter 8.

Wave Shoaling

Figure 3.5 shows an idealized "snapshot" view of the changes in wave height, length, water particle motion, and average water level that occur when waves move into shallow water. In deep water, water particles move in vertical orbits that decrease rapidly with depth; water particle motion due to deep-water waves is nearly zero at depths greater than half the wave length. As waves approach the shore, water particle motion extends to the bottom, and the orbits become elliptical in shape. As the wave progresses into shallower water, the elliptic paths of the water particles do not close and the water particles advance a short distance in the direction of wave motion with each passing wave crest. Accompanying these changes in the water motion are changes in the wave form; the crests become sharply peaked and the troughs broader and shallower relative to still water level. With further shoaling the waves become so steep and unstable that they break; and this occurs approximately at the point where the water depth is 1.25 to 2.20 times the wave height. Just prior to breaking, waves travel almost entirely above the still water level and the water particles move onshore in arc-shaped surges. The shoreward motion of water particles due to wave breaking causes a current to flow in the surf zone parallel to the shore in the direction of wave travel. This is called the longshore current and it is the major agent that moves sand along a beach.

Wave energy dissipation is completed when the waves run up the beach in a sheetlike flow and percolate into it. Wave runup can supply large volumes of water to the upper beach during storms and is a flood hazard in low coastal areas. The zone of wave transformation may be only a few meters wide in protected waters, but along the exposed beaches of the Strait of Juan de Fuca it can be more than 100 meters (328 feet) wide during storms.

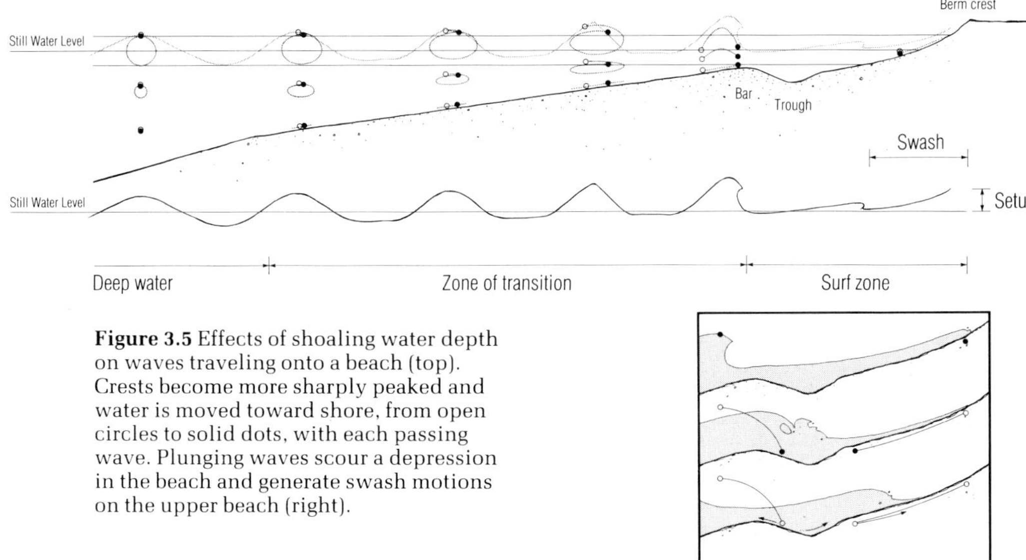

Figure 3.5 Effects of shoaling water depth on waves traveling onto a beach (top). Crests become more sharply peaked and water is moved toward shore, from open circles to solid dots, with each passing wave. Plunging waves scour a depression in the beach and generate swash motions on the upper beach (right).

Refraction and Diffraction

There is another very important effect of shoaling. Waves that approach a shore at an angle tend to be refracted, or rotated, so their crests become parallel with the coastline. Refraction is easily visualized with a simple ray path or refraction diagram. Wave rays are imaginary lines perpendicular to wave crests (Fig. 3.6). Wave energy travels in the direction of these rays, thus a refraction diagram illustrates variations in the direction of energy transfer as waves approach the beach. Areas on the shore where wave rays converge receive more wave energy and will have higher breaker heights than areas where rays diverge. Because of refraction, wave energy is concentrated at headlands and diminished in bays.

These effects are illustrated in the refraction diagrams of 8- and 12-second ocean swell at Ediz Hook. The 12-second swell is long, about 225 meters (740 feet), and is affected by the shoaling bottom at the 370-foot depth contour. The prominent outward bulge in the bottom focuses the wave energy on the base of Ediz Hook but defocuses it at the end of the spit. The 8-second waves are not refracted until they are very close to shore. Since they are about half as long as the 12-second swell their energy is spread more evenly along the spit.

Stacks, jetties, and small islands which pierce the water surface produce another wave phenomenon, called diffraction. This is the phenomenon by which waves travel around an object or through a narrow gap between objects and spread into the sheltered region behind them. It is an important consideration in the siting of structures on the coast. An example of diffraction patterns around a small island is shown in an air photo of Crescent Bay, Clallam County.

Refraction

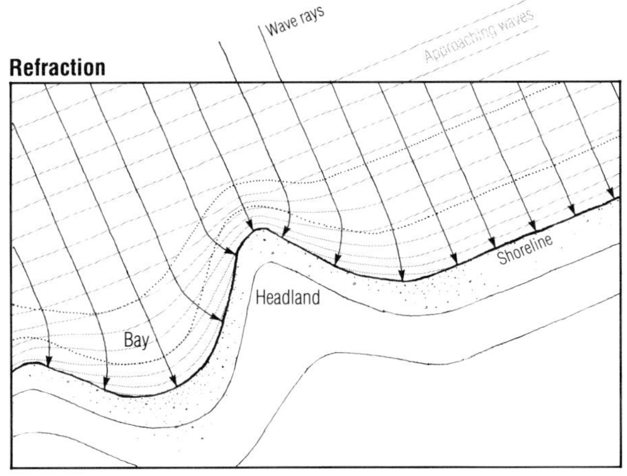

Figure 3.6 Top: Refraction of waves at a coast focuses wave energy on headlands and spreads it in bays. Middle: Long period waves with greater length are more strongly refracted by offshore bathymetry than short waves. Bottom: Wave diffraction into a marina and an inlet, and around an island.

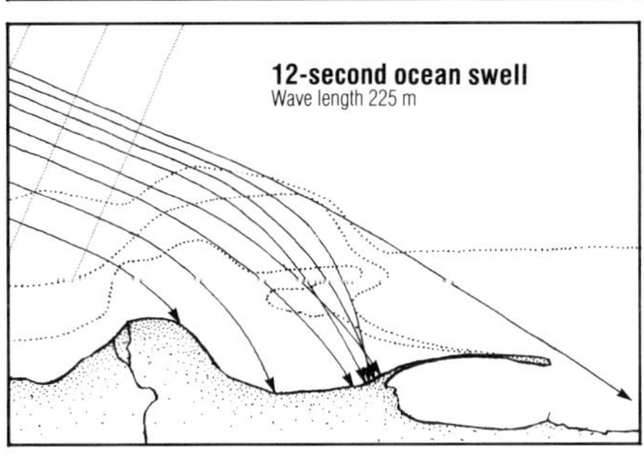

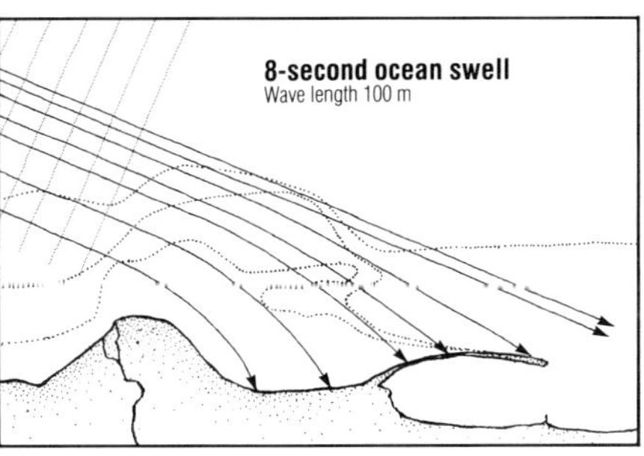

Diffraction

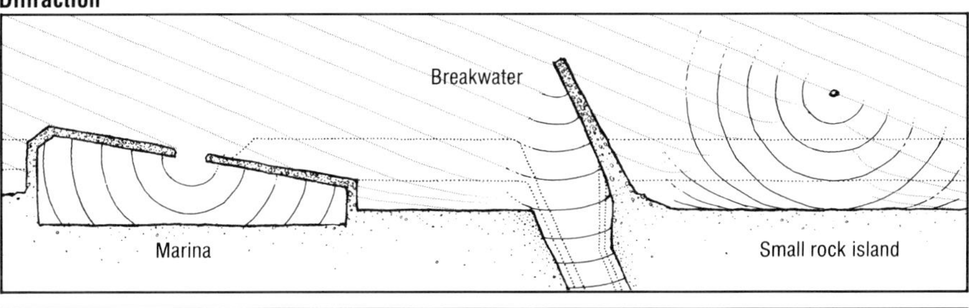

Wave crest patterns in Crescent Bay, Clallam County, produced by diffraction around an island and wave refraction on the beach.

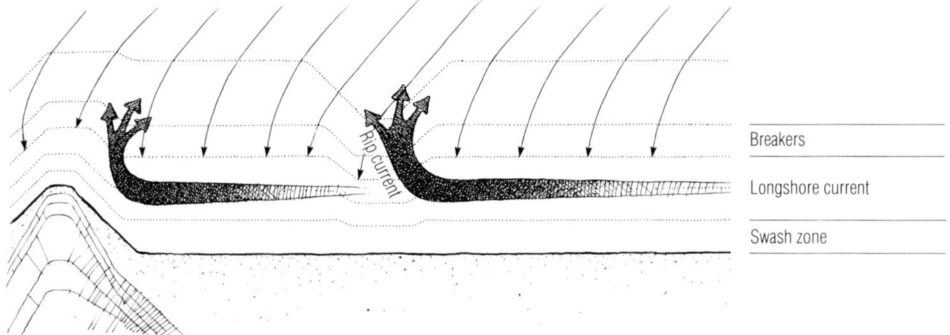

Figure 3.7 Longshore currents generated by waves breaking on a beach. Rip currents develop where longshore currents are deflected offshore by a headland or where wave heights are diminished.

Nearshore Currents

One of the more important effects associated with wave shoaling (Fig. 3.5) is the transport of water toward the beach by breaking waves. Shoaling waves push water onshore in much the same way that pressure moves water through other simple hydraulic systems such as pipes and open channels. One result is that water accumulates on the beach face, producing an elevated water level called setup. Setup can be as much as twenty percent of the breaker height. When the waves break at a small angle to the beach, part of the pressure is directed parallel with the beach and creates a longshore current (Fig. 3.7).

Longshore currents flow along the beach in the same general direction that the waves are moving; and the current speed is determined by the angle between breaker crests and the shoreline, as well as the wave height. An estimate of the speed and direction of the longshore current can be made easily by tossing a slightly buoyant object into the surf zone near the breaker line and noting the average rate and direction of travel down the beach as it oscillates with the passing waves. This simple experiment should be performed at slack water so that tidal currents are not included in the measurement.

Water moved onshore by waves does not accumulate indefinitely on the beach, and a nearshore circulation cell is established in which water moves shoreward in portions of the cell and seaward in others to maintain a balance alongshore. Nearshore water moves parallel with the beach as a longshore current, and then returns offshore as a rip current. Rip currents are one means by which water is returned offshore beyond the surf zone. They form where breaker heights are low due to refraction, or where there is an obstacle to longshore flow. They are narrow and swift where they penetrate the breaker line and can erode channels in the beach sediment. But once outside the breakers they spread laterally and decrease in speed quite rapidly. Rip currents are accompanied by foam lines and discoloration of the water by wave-sus-

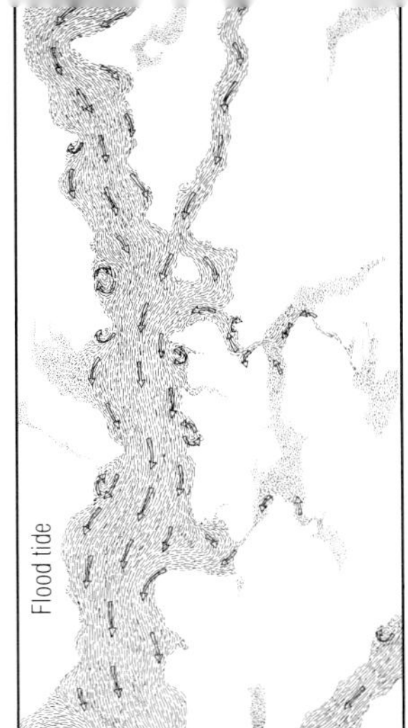

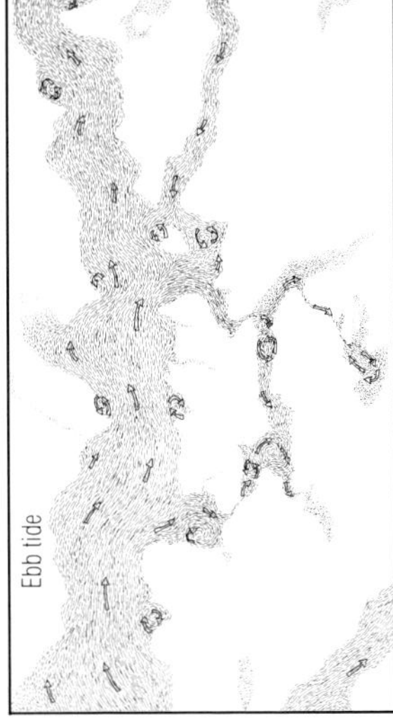

Figure 3.8 Surface currents in the main basin of Puget Sound during flood and ebb tides as simulated in a hydraulic model. Tidal currents are weak in the heads of bays and swift in channels connecting large basins. The phase of the tide is shown below.

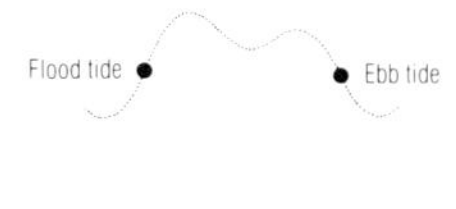

pended sediment. They may extend up to 200–300 meters seaward on the exposed beaches along the Strait of Juan de Fuca but are more commonly much shorter, less than 50 meters, on beaches in the Sound.

Tidal Currents

Currents in Puget Sound are driven predominantly by the semidiurnal (twice daily) tide. In the major basins and passes of Puget Sound, the swiftest surface currents flow in the channel centers. Tidal currents move slowly near shore because of bottom friction, especially along coastal sectors with broad shallow areas offshore from the beach. The weaker tidal flows do not move much sediment in the shallow areas near shore. The exception occurs at the ends of the major points, Point Robinson, West Point, Point No Point, and Point Wilson, for example, and along the shores of narrow passes such as Deception Pass, Port Townsend Canal, and Agate Pass that connect basins where large volumes of water move as the tide rises and falls. Strong flows through these channels extend onto the beach during high tide and move sand and fine gravel without wave agitation.

The complex surface current patterns that are produced by the tides and the topography of Puget Sound can be visualized with the aid of physical or computer models. Several features occur in tidal flow which affect sedimentation patterns in Puget Sound. These are illustrated by the current chart shown in Figure 3.8. These patterns were recorded by photographing small particles moving on the surface of a model of Puget Sound at various phases of the tide. It is clear from the flow patterns that tidal currents are weak in the heads of most bays—these are areas of rapid deposition of mud and organic debris. The strong currents and large eddies formed at points of land and narrow passes are also evident—these areas of faster currents typically have coarse bottom sediments, sand, and gravel, as the current speed and turbulence is sufficient to prevent deposition of fine particles.

CHAPTER 4

Sediment Transport

Sediment movement nearshore is the direct cause of many problems that affect coastal development in Puget Sound. Some are simple and easily solved but others are considerably more complex, have costly solutions, and may require expensive maintenance programs. Shoaling in the shallow harbors at Olympia and Shelton and destructive erosion of developed spits such as Ediz Hook, for example, interfere with commerce and the use of shore property. It is necessary to understand how waves and currents move sediments in order to solve these kinds of problems.

In order for people's coastal activities and developments to coexist sensibly with the constantly shifting patterns of nearshore erosion and deposition, the nearby sediment sources, sinks, and transport pathways must be identified. Clearly, it is not wise to develop commercial port facilities in waters where large volumes of sediment accumulate, such as the head of a bay, or to site a home on an unstable sandy bluff or on an eroding spit. In the past, siting and construction decisions have been based upon local knowledge of the sedimentation patterns in a coastal area and quite frequently they were correct. New developments, however, now occur in areas of Puget Sound which are inappropriate for a planned usage or where local knowledge is unreliable simply because existing information covers a short time span. Key project decisions in the future will necessitate more complex engineering evaluations than ever before. The basis for these evaluations consists largely of ideas about sediment transport acquired from studies conducted in other parts of the world and must be adapted to the Puget Sound region.

A concept that is often useful when considering coastal sedimentation and its effects on development is the transport cell. A transport cell is a segment of the shore that includes a source of sediment, an area where it accumulates, and a connecting path between the two. In the Sound transport cells usually consist of eroding bluffs that supply sediment to a spit, tombolo, or other growing deposit downdrift (Fig. 4.1). In these transport cells, the beaches connecting the bluffs with the deposit provide the pathway for sediment movement. The important attribute that distinguishes sources and sinks from the transport pathways is that pathways neither contribute nor remove sediment from the sys-

Figure 4.1 Sediment transport cell, Heron Island, Pierce County. Waves from the south remove sand and gravel from the bluffs (source) and transport it along the beach (pathway) to a spit in deeper water (sink).

tem. They only conduct it and little long-term erosion or deposition occurs in them.

In the absence of historical data on river channel stability, bluff erosion rates, and shoaling patterns for an area, the identification of transport cells is difficult. Relationships between the local oceanographic conditions and the coastal geology are aids in the identification process. The key parameters in most situations include the current speeds, the height and directional characteristics of the waves typical of the area, and the particle size of the sediments that cover the seabed. The purpose of this section is to summarize the important relationships among these factors.

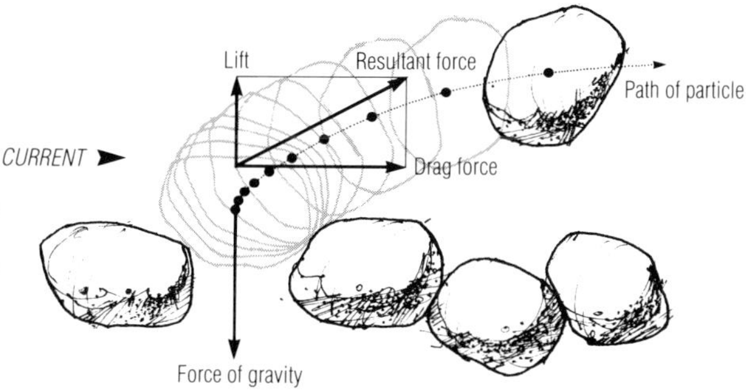

Figure 4.2 Forces that move a grain of sand as it is scoured from the sea bed by a current.

Forces on the Seabed

Water flowing over loose sediment particles on the seabed exerts a force on them which includes direct pressure on the upstream sides of the particle, as well as lift due to water flowing rapidly over the tops of the particles (Fig. 4.2). The roughness of the seabed, the intensity of turbulence near the bottom, and average flow speed determine how large these forces will be. In a very general way, they vary with average flow speed squared; that is, a two-fold increase in flow speed produces a four-fold increase in force, and a three-fold increase produces a nine-fold increase in force, and so on. The result of these combined forces is that when the lift force on a sediment grain exceeds the gravitational force holding it down on the seabed, it will be suspended and transported downstream. The water speed necessary to move sediment is called the erosion velocity. Figure 4.3 shows that the erosion velocity

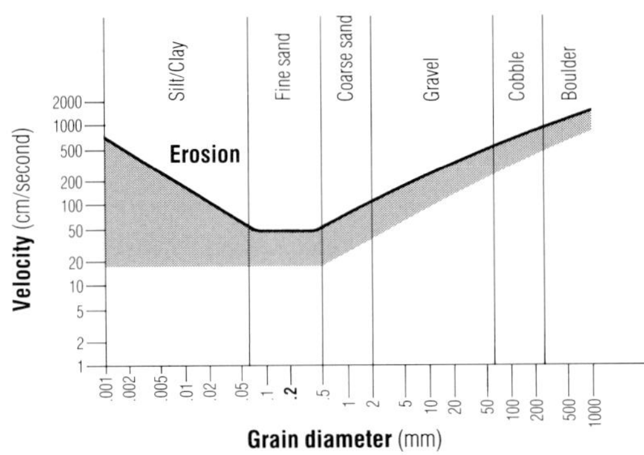

Figure 4.3 Range of current velocities (shaded area) and maximum velocity (solid line) required to erode sediment grains of various diameters.

increases with grain size for most sizes. The erosion velocity for silt and clay is highly variable, however, because of the cohesiveness resulting from chemical and biological activity in these materials. Sediment cohesion can cause silts and clays to be very resistant to erosion by currents. For example, cohesive mud on a tidal flat can resist erosion by a current of up to 300 centimeters per second (9.8 feet per second) but this same current could easily erode 10.0-millimeter (0.4-inch) gravel.

Transport Modes

Once in motion, the vertical distribution of sediments in the water column is determined by flow turbulence and the settling rates of the sediment particles. Flow turbulence and particle settling counteract one another; turbulence diffuses sediment upwards, whereas settling tends to return it to the seabed. Settling rates are determined by particle size, density, and shape. Both processes, diffusion and settling, occur together so that sediment is continually maintained in suspension. The forces exerted on the seabed can provide an estimate of the turbulence intensity, as well as the tendency of the flow to be uniformly loaded or mixed with sediment.

As an illustration of the effects of turbulence and particle settling on the distribution of sediment suspended in a flow, consider a channel two meters (6.6 feet) deep in which current velocities can be made to change, say from 0 to 150 centimeters per second (4.9 feet per second), and the bed can be composed of silt, sand, or gravel. Silt will be suspended and well mixed throughout the water column for the full range of flow speeds. Gravel, on the other hand, can be suspended only a few centimeters above the bed by a current of 150 centimeters per second. Figure 4.4a shows these effects graphically.

Wherever the flow speed exceeds the erosion velocity for a given particle size the particles are transported. Silt and clay are easily held in suspension because they settle slowly and are transported as suspended load. They also get uniformly mixed throughout the water column over a wide range of flow speeds. Coarse sand and gravel roll along the bottom as bedload since suspension requires currents swifter than 150 centimeters per second. Fine to medium sand is transported in one or both modes depending on current speed. A 24-centimeter per second (0.8-foot per second) current moves sand as bedload, but currents swifter than 60 centimeters per second (2.0 feet per second) move sand in suspension as well. The transport of sediment in suspension is a very efficient process, as is shown on Figure 4.4b. For example, a 40-centimeter per second (1.3-foot per second) current moves about 100 times more fine sand as suspended load than as bedload.

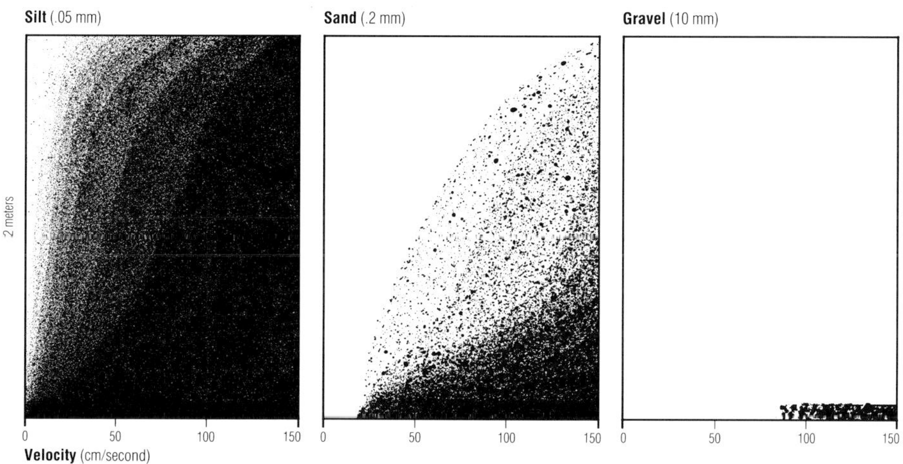

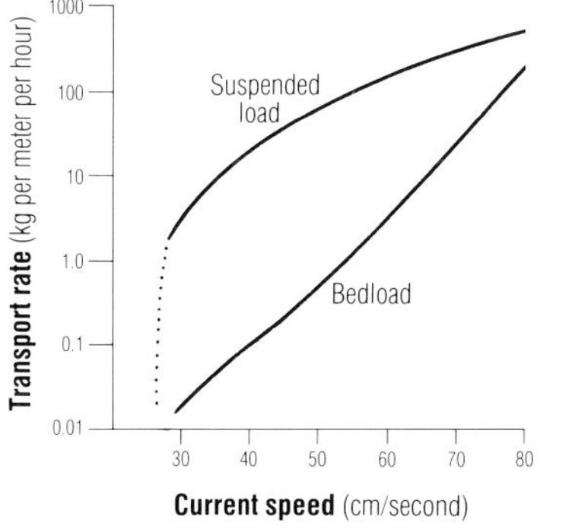

Figure 4.4 A. Above: Vertical distribution of silt, sand, and gravel in a tidal channel, two meters deep, with different current speeds. B. Left: Variation of suspended load and bedload of fine sand with current speed. At current speeds less than 30 cm/second, suspended load decreases rapidly, as indicated by the dotted curve.

Currents and Waves Together

The principles of sediment suspension and transport by steady currents apply quite well, even when wave motion occurs with the currents. The hydraulic forces that lift sediment off the seabed and mix it into the water are the same. Waves alone transport sediment inefficiently because they move it to and fro without net motion as is produced by a steady current. Wave motion and currents acting together on the seabed, however, are much more effective in transporting sediment than currents alone for several reasons.

- When waves and currents occur together, they exert larger forces on the seabed than would be expected from the simple addition of wave and current forces considered separately.
- Wave-induced turbulence produces more complete mixing of suspended sediment into the water column.
- Sediment, once suspended by waves, can be transported by currents of only a few centimeters per second.

A sketch of the second and third effects is shown in Figure 4.5.

On the beach, breaking waves transport water in the direction of wave travel, creating a longshore current and sediment transport along the beach. Engineers use the significant wave height to estimate the longshore current speed and the rate of sand transport along the shore. Figure 4.6 indicates that as wave height and period and the breaker angle become larger the rate of sand transport increases. The scatter of data points about the design curve relating sand transport and wave energy flux demonstrates the high degree of uncertainty in predicting sand transport on beaches by this method. Much of Puget Sound is not exposed to ocean waves to which these principles are best applied. Instead, the waves are short and break suddenly on the sloping part of the beach face. These waves produce sediment motion in a very narrow zone by a process called beach drifting. In beach drifting, sediment is rolled along the beach in a zig-zag path as illustrated in Figure 4.5. Considerable caution must be exercised in designing structures that influence coastal processes. When available, other data can provide more reliable estimates of sand transport rates. These include: (1) actual measurements of transport rates from a nearby site, (2) historical changes in coastal features recorded by sequences of old charts or photographs, and (3) past dredging records indicating shoaling and erosion rates.

Sediment Budgets

It is often useful to establish a sediment budget for a coastal area when solving sediment problems. Additions of material to a nearshore region are balanced against losses to determine if the region is gaining or losing material; an excess of material supplied over losses indicates deposition is occurring, whereas erosion results if losses exceed the supply. In balancing the budget, sediment cannot be created or destroyed within the area—all of it must be accounted for in some way.

For this purpose, a simple box can be envisioned at the project site that encloses the problem area (Fig. 4.7). The sides of the box must extend from the sea surface down to the depth affected by the project un-

Surf zone

Figure 4.5 The process of sand suspension under a breaking wave. Intense turbulence under the plunging wave scours a shallow trough in the beach. Sand and gravel are carried up the beach face by the swash and roll down the beach in the backwash.

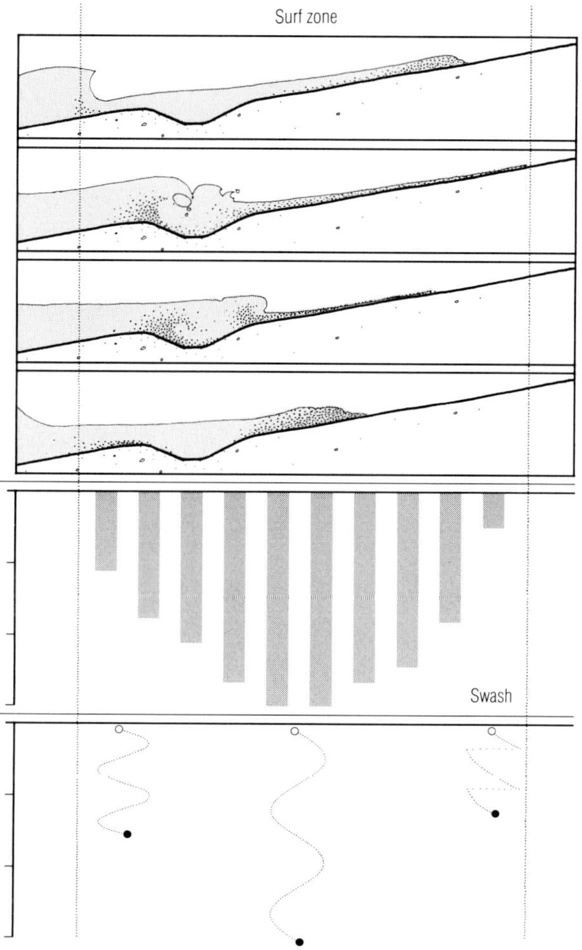

Longshore current speeds vary nearshore; the higher current speeds occur in the middle of the surf zone.

Swash

Waves and longshore currents transport sediment along oscillating paths. The rolling motion in the swash is called beach drifting.

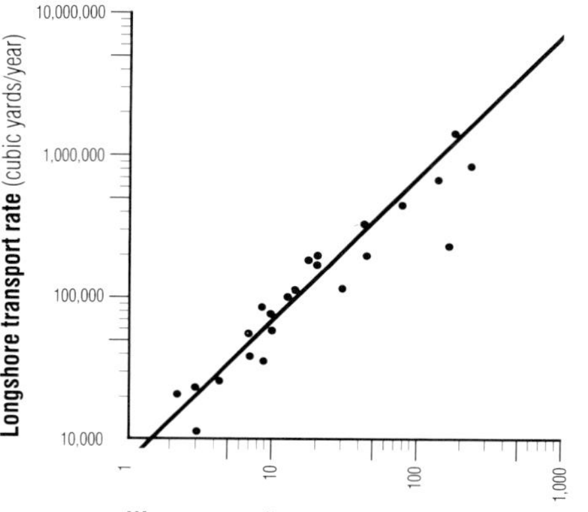

Figure 4.6 A graph for estimating longshore sand transport rates from wave energy flux.

Figure 4.7 Sediment budget for a segment of coast. Inputs include longshore and onshore transport, bluff erosion, and beach nourishment; outputs result from beach erosion and longshore transport.

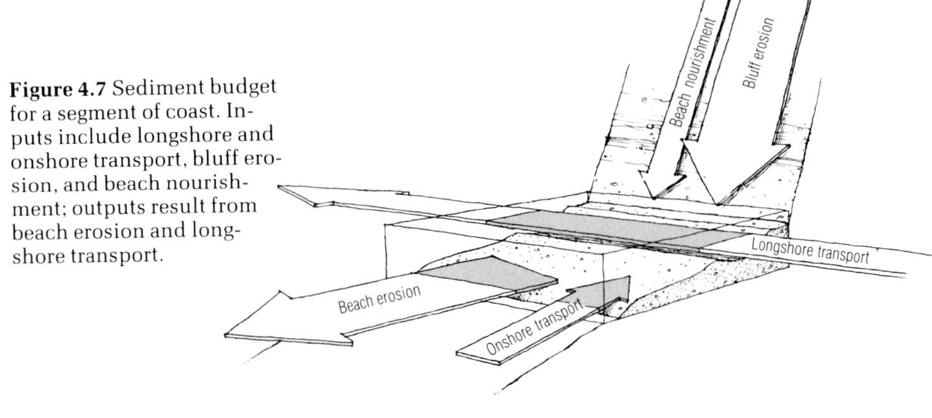

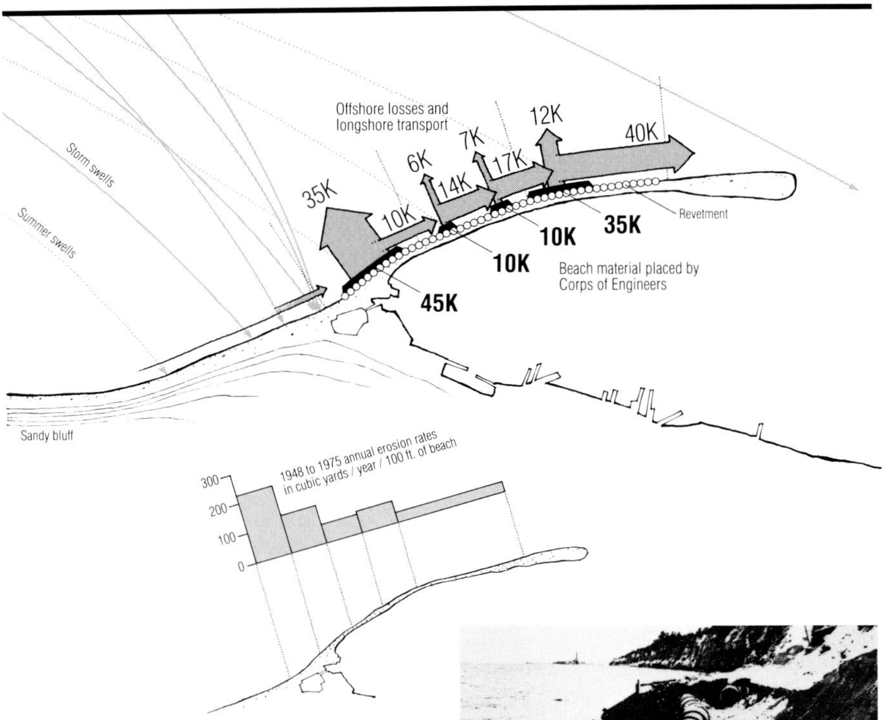

Figure 4.8 Sediment budgets (top) and erosion rates (middle) at Ediz Hook. Bold numbers are volumes of material added to the beach; light numbers are volumes of material eroded. Right: Beach erosion west of Ediz Hook and remedy prior to the Corps of Engineers beach nourishment program.

der evaluation. The principal natural sources of sediment to the box are bluff erosion, rivers, and littoral drift from the updrift coast. Major losses result from wave action and pass through the downdrift and seaward boundaries of the control box. Other gains and losses are man-caused and are important when development plans include dredging or structures such as jetties, groins, or seawalls that alter the natural flow of sediment through the area.

There are many applications of this simple notion to real coastal problems. When the inputs and outputs to the box are known, impacts of man-made structures on deposition and erosion can be predicted with confidence. When the inputs and outputs are unknown, measurements of the erosion and deposition rates can be used to estimate them.

Recent shore protection work at Ediz Hook by the Corps of Engineers illustrates some of the potentials of this approach. Ediz Hook is a large spit that protects the harbor at Port Angeles. Prior to 1930 the spit was a stable feature because an adequate supply of beach material from eroding bluffs to the west offset the constant removal of material by wave action. During 1930, a water main protected by a 732 meter (2,400-foot) bulkhead was built at the base of the bluffs to supply water to the forest products facility located on the west end of Ediz Hook. This development stabilized the bluff but also reduced the supply of beach material to the spit. With the sediment supply cut off erosion of the exposed beaches became a serious problem (Fig. 4.8). In 1958–1961 the problem was aggravated when additional shore protection was installed. Since then the beaches have been eroded to the point where storm waves have caused major damage to the service roads near the base of the spit in recent years.

The restoration of Ediz Hook included the placement of continuous revetment, an embankment of stone or concrete, along the beach at the base of the spit by the Corps of Engineers and periodic replenishment of eroded beach material to preserve the aesthetic and recreational qualities of the shore and to protect the toe of the revetment wall.

In 1975, the Corps of Engineers conducted experiments to determine the optimal composition of beach feed material and replenishment rates required on Ediz Hook. In these studies, they determined a suitable budget of beach material that would assure a stable beach profile. Since the exact littoral drift rates and offshore losses of beach material were not known, the dispersal of test material was monitored at four locations along the spit. Using these data and mean annual erosion rates acquired from longer term surveys (1948–1970), the offshore losses and longshore transport rates were estimated (Fig. 4.8). An interesting aspect of the sediment budget for Ediz Hook is the increase in the longshore transport along the spit. This occurs because at the base of the spit the angle of wave approach is nearly perpendicular to the

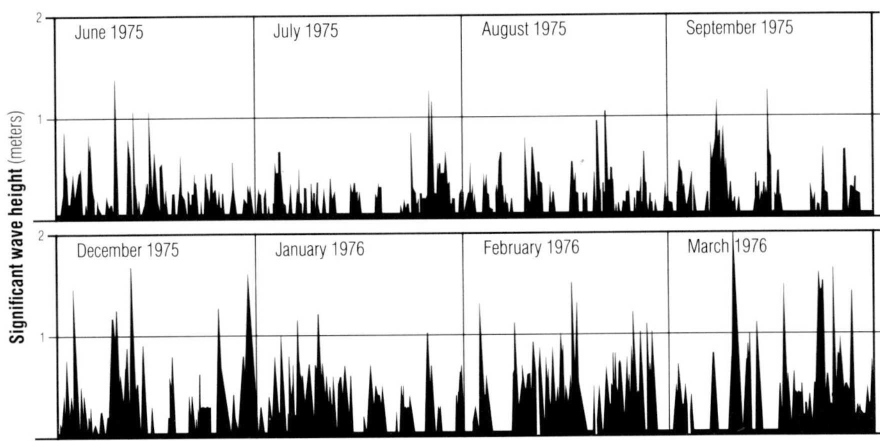

Figure 4.9 Wave heights recorded at White Rock, B.C. Storms and wave heights exceeding one meter (solid lines across graphs) occur most frequently during winter months.

beach but decreases toward the end, resulting in stronger longshore currents and more sediment transport there.

The problems at Ediz Hook emphasize the importance of considering sediment source, transport path, and sink as three identifiable parts to a longshore transport cell and the impact of beach modifications that alter one or more of these parts. The success of the rehabilitation of Ediz Hook will be an important advance in erosion control using the natural transport system.

Beach Profiles

The nearshore zone is constantly undergoing change in response to the weather, stage of the tide, and wave conditions. Since longshore transport is usually driven by waves, beach profiles respond most strongly to fluctuations in wave conditions. Wave height and direction change over time scales of hours, in response to storms, and seasonally as well.

Puget Sound winters are characterized by frequent storms and large waves (Fig. 4.9). Longshore currents transport substantially greater sediment loads along the shore; the beach face is eroded, and a high berm forms in response to the strong swash associated with large waves and high spring tides. The sediment on the beach face tends to be coarser in winter because the finer sediments are carried offshore or downdrift by wave action to a less exposed beach. The storm profile most prevalent in winter months is sketched in Figure 4.10.

With the onset of spring and through the summer months, storm wave activity diminishes, light northerly winds prevail, and beaches

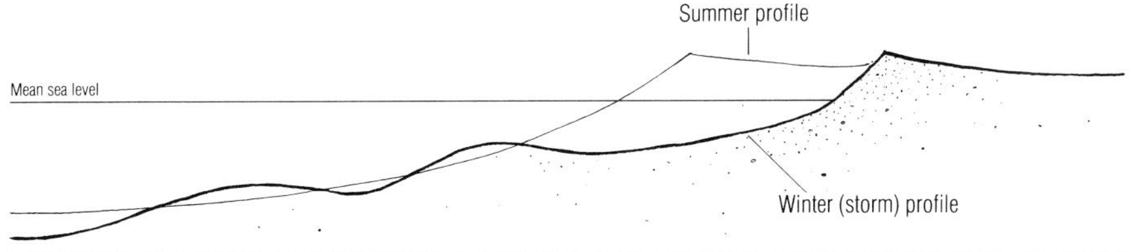

Figure 4.10 Summer and winter beach profiles develop as beach sediment moves onshore and offshore during an annual cycle.

tend to rebuild a low-wave or "summer" profile (Fig. 4.10). Sand is transported to the beach from deposits formed offshore during storms. Deposition of finer material occurs on the beach face and a new berm is constructed reflecting low-wave conditions and the completion of the annual cycle. Although there is great variability in the storm frequency from year to year, these trends are nonetheless observable most years.

Many beaches in Puget Sound are composed of lag gravel which is sufficiently erosion resistant that the seasonal profile variations are slight. The only perceptible seasonal change is the deposition of a thin veneer of sand, usually less than 10 centimeters (4 inches) thick, on the beach face during the summer followed by its disappearance in winter.

In many areas an additional annual cycle is a major change in wave direction in response to seasonal wind patterns (Fig. 6.1, p. 62). This change can cause the area of sand deposition to shift along a beach. Many of the north–south oriented beaches in Puget Sound show this condition. Winter storms produce southerly winds and waves, and sand movement is from south to north along the beach. During the winter, coarse sediments often accumulate along the southern side of logs, small groins, stairways, and boat ramps that extend across the beach. During summer, northerly winds prevail, causing sand to migrate onshore and to the south along these beaches. This causes sand to accumulate on the north side of any structures or logs that cross the beach face. People who live along the shore observe these changes in orientations and beach profile as the natural cycle of events in the nearshore zone. These changes are taken up in the next chapter.

Figure 5.1 Evolution of a gravel and cobble beach over geologic time. Erosion of glacial material and longshore transport was rapid during initial stages (5,000 to 1,000 years before present, but decreased sediment supply in recent time has resulted in narrow beaches of lag gravel and cobbles. Right: Sea level since the last glaciation.

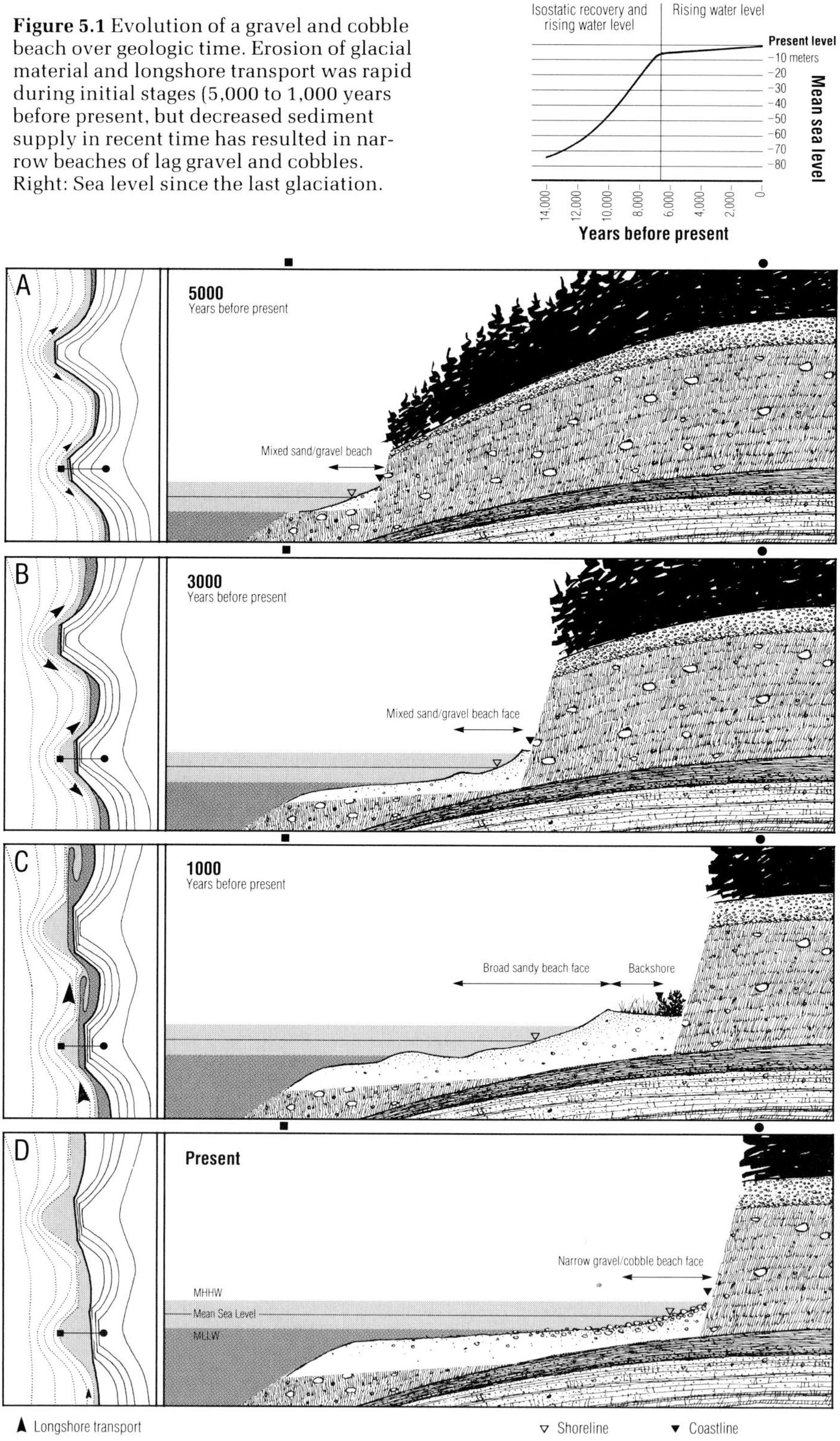

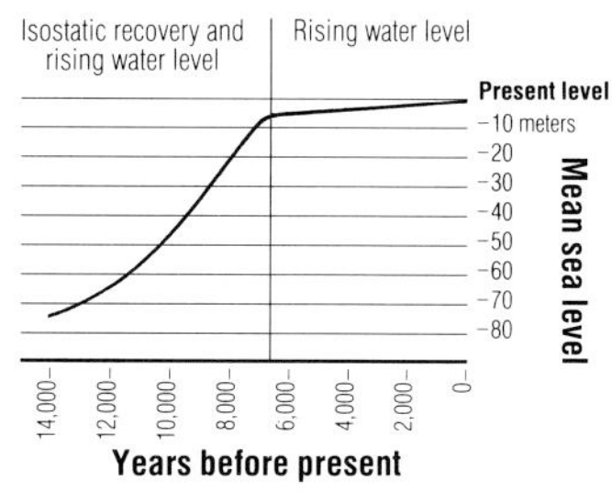

A

5000
Years before present

Mixed sand/gravel beach

B

3000
Years before present

Mixed sand/gravel beach face

C

1000
Years before present

Broad sandy beach face

Backshore

D

Present

Narrow gravel/cobble beach face

MHHW

Mean Sea Level

MLLW

▲ Longshore transport

▽ Shoreline

▼ Coastline

CHAPTER 5

More on Beaches
The Details

Gravel-Cobble Beaches

Because steep shore bluffs with adjacent gravel and cobble beaches are so common in Puget Sound, a simple picture model is given in Figure 5.1 which illustrates the successive stages of their geological development. The model depicts the dispersal of sediment from glacial deposits by waves and currents to nearshore deposits, spits, bars, and beaches. This process is a completely natural one, but as will become clear in subsequent chapters, development activities and man-made structures can interfere with certain aspects of it.

The sea cliffs and bluffs that surround Puget Sound today did not exist 5,000 years ago. Instead, much of the coastal terrain at that time was probably smooth and rounded like the present upland areas of the central Puget lowlands.

The beaches in the initial phase of formation might have resembled the one sketched in Figure 5.1a. With time, the coastline moved progressively landward as waves removed material from the uplands. Erosion rates varied greatly from one location to another throughout the Sound depending on wave climate and cliff stability, and the rate of cliff recession depicted in the model is somewhat arbitrary. After cliff erosion has proceeded for some time, a small beach develops from material eroded from the headlands (5.1b), and a narrow low-tide terrace, cut into glacial material, extends offshore from the beach. At this phase, cliffs exist on prominent headlands exposed to wave erosion; and longshore currents carry sediment away from the headlands to bays on either side. Since the cliff face is bounded by deep bays on both sides, the entire sediment supply to the beach comes from the local cliff. Also the low-tide terrace is too narrow to dissipate much wave energy before it arrives at the beach. Consequently, sediment is removed from the base of the cliff at nearly the same rate it accumulates there.

With continued erosion of headlands, the coastline is straightened and wave attack on the shore is continuous along extensive segments of the coast. Sediment is now supplied to beaches by longshore currents from remote sources. The low-tide terrace is wider and wave energy at the cliff base is reduced, particularly at the lower phases of the tide (Fig. 5.1c). This is a healthy phase of beach evolution in Puget Sound.

There is a plentiful supply of sand along major segments of the coast; cliff erosion rates are lower than during the preceding phase because wave energy is dissipated on broad low-tide terraces, and abundant beach material lies at the base of the sea cliffs. Well-nourished beaches are effective wave buffers and beach plant communities and wetlands can form behind them. Examples of these shores exist along some exposed sections of the west side of Whidbey Island from Ebey's Landing south to Bush Point.

Figure 5.1d depicts a beach in a state of decay. The volume of material at the cliff base is decreased greatly. The beach has lost most of its sand and consists largely of gravel and cobbles, which form an armorlike surface on the beach face and parts of the low-tide terrace. This beach is not particularly attractive nor enjoyable to walk upon because it is rough and lacks a broad dry berm. Since there is no backshore, the beach face is usually submerged at high tide and is of limited recreational value. Gravel beaches without backshores are the result of an inadequate sediment supply and may indicate coastal erosion. The construction of bulkheads, revetment, groins, and other structures to stabilize sea cliffs reduces the sediment supply to downdrift beaches; and in many instances these measures have remedied one condition but aggravated another because of man-caused reductions of sediment supply. Beaches in this condition are becoming more prevalent in Puget Sound, especially along highly developed and modified sections of the coast.

Coastal Sediments

Careful observation of beach sediments exposed at low tide reveals subtle differences in their characteristics from one location to another. Beach sediment may originate from the terrestrial or marine environment. Rivers, erosion of upland sediments and cliffs, and wind-blown sand are terrestrial; shells, animal body parts, and sandbars are marine.

Two of these sources, rivers and cliff erosion, dominate beach sedimentation in Puget Sound. It is estimated that 3.2 million metric tons (3.5 million short tons) of sediment enter Puget Sound from major rivers and that another 2.7 million metric tons (3.0 million short tons) come from beach and cliff erosion every year. Ninety percent of the river input is fine-grained material that does not form deposits on most beaches. Therefore, beach and cliff erosion are the primary sources of beach sediment.

From a distance all beach sediment looks very similar, but its characteristics strongly reflect the physical and biological processes active on a beach. These characteristics include: (1) the proportion of biological to detrital material (shell fragments versus mineral grains and rock fragments); (2) sediment color (dark versus light minerals); and (3)

Figure 5.2 Left: Classification of sediments by grain diameter. Right: A sampler of beach sediments from Puget Sound: upper left, boulders; upper right, mixture of cobbles and coarse sand; middle left, cobbles and gravel; middle right, gravel, shell, and coarse sand; lower left, gravel; lower right, fine sand and shell.

Grain diameter (mm)	
	Boulder
256.0	
	Cobble
64.0	
	Gravel
2.0	
	Coarse sand
0.5	
	Fine sand
0.062	
	Silt/clay
0.001	

grain size (gravel versus sand) (Fig. 5.2). The predominant grain size is related to the magnitude of wave energy dissipated on the beach while mineral composition suggests the source material and, in some instances, the pathway followed by the sediment from its source to the beach.

Mineral Composition

Glacial material on the beach originated from the igneous, metamorphic, and sedimentary rocks of the Coast Mountains in British Columbia and the northern Cascade Range. Streams and rivers draining Quaternary deposits and volcanic terrain in the Cascade and Olympic ranges also contribute to the variety of sediment that is supplied to the beaches.

Unlike many open ocean beaches in the temperate latitudes with sand of light-colored mineral grains, Puget Sound beaches consist of darker materials. These materials are sands composed of:

- plagioclase feldspar and hornblende (dark minerals);
- volcanic rock fragments weathered from the Cascade volcanoes (Mts. Baker, Rainier, and Glacier Peak);
- marine basalt fragments from the Olympic Peninsula.

Beach cobbles and boulders are composed primarily of:

- gray-green volcanic rock;
- dark and light-banded gneiss;
- light-colored granitic rock.

More exotic materials can be found in localized deposits; the striking red and pink sand and gravel of ribbon chert at Lopez Island and the garnet-rich sand in Tulalip and Livingston bays are but two examples.

Clam diggers are no doubt familiar with the layered appearance of sediment deposits on beaches and in sandbars exposed at low tide. Figure 5.3 shows a shallow trench dug into the beach face. The horizontal beds intersecting with the onshore sloped layers (cross-bedding) record the migration of a longshore bar up the beach face. The alternating dark and light layers result from variations in the amount of dark-colored minerals in the sand composing each layer. These features record the sorting of dark- and light-colored minerals on the beach because of the unique hydraulic characteristics resulting from their size, shape, and density. Grains with similar hydraulic characteristics, notably settling speed, move together and form deposits at the same location under certain wave conditions.

Figure 5.3 Trench in a beach exposed to large waves. Sorting of sediment by size and density produces layering; sandbar movement produces intersecting layers.

Sediment Size

Grain size is of more practical concern than color or composition because several engineering properties of beaches, notably load bearing capacity and permeability, depend on it. A classification scheme for sediment grains according to their diameter is given in Figure 5.2. Many boulders scattered about the shores of Puget Sound were emplaced originally by glacial ice and are too heavy to be moved by waves. Others have rolled onto the beach from upland outcrops of bedrock or till. They provide sand-starved beaches with a measure of erosion protection because they dissipate wave energy which might otherwise erode material from the backshore and adjacent bluffs. Boulders also

Table 5.1 Distribution of beach sediment types by county. Table entries are in square kilometers and percentages are of the total coastal area.

Region	County	Rock	Gravel	Sand	Mud/Sand	Mud
Western	Clallam	2.5	7.1	14.6	0.0	0.2
	Jefferson	<0.1	8.6	5.8	2.4	0.3
	Mason	<0.1	7.4	2.3	11.3	4.1
	Thurston	0.0	2.7	6.5	1.5	6.3
	Total	2.5	25.8	29.2	15.2	10.9
		<1%	**8%**	**9%**	**5%**	**3%**
Central	Snohomish	0.0	0.8	3.8	15.2	17.7
	King	0.0	3.5	7.3	0.3	<0.1
	Kitsap	0.3	32.9	13.8	1.5	3.5
	Pierce	<0.1	7.1	4.3	1.7	4.6
	Total	0.4	44.3	29.2	18.7	25.9
		<1%	**13%**	**9%**	**6%**	**8%**
Northern	Whatcom	0.2	2.2	7.8	11.1	1.9
	Skagit	0.2	5.1	1.4	39.0	15.2
	San Juan	1.5	4.4	4.3	0.4	<0.1
	Island	<0.1	6.7	18.5	16.6	0.2
	Total	2.0	18.4	32.0	67.1	17.3
		<1%	**5%**	**9%**	**20%**	**5%**
Combined total		**<1%**	**26%**	**27%**	**31%**	**16%**

trap drift logs which provide additional erosion protection. Table 5.1 gives the occurrence of sediment types by area and percentages in each county.

Sediments at the other end of the size spectrum, the silts and clays, form deposits only in areas protected from wave activity and strong tidal currents. Clay, silt, and fine sand, collectively called the fine material of nearshore sediment, are too easily suspended and moved about by weak currents to remain on the beach for long. Once silts and clays have settled to the seabed during periods of slack current and calm seas, however, they can form a cohesive mud deposit that is quite resistant to erosion by tidal currents. When mud is further stabilized by fibrous plant material, it forms deposits that are surprisingly resistant to erosion even by storm waves.

Sediments that accumulate nearshore have a range of grain sizes which is determined by the level of wave and current activity and the size of sediment available for transport. Along the shores from Whidbey Island to southern Puget Sound it is common to have a range of sediment sizes from clay to cobbles available for transport by waves. These particles become sorted by size as they move through the nearshore zone. The fines are winnowed out of the initial material and carried by nearshore currents to calm waters away from the exposed part of the beach. Sand and gravel are moved less easily, however, and remain on the wave-exposed beach, migrating along the shore in response to waves and currents. The coarse gravels and cobbles are even more resistant to movement by waves and commonly form an armor on the face of a sand-starved beach. Often within this armor deposit fine materials can accumulate because they are protected from wave action

Table 5.2 Classification of coastal features based on erosion and deposition.

Coastal Features	Beaches and Sediment Characteristics	Locations where features are common
Depositional	**Various major morphological features produced by a large supply of sediment deposited in a nearshore area. (Examples, pages 10 and 12)**	
River deltas	• Variety of sediment types from mud to gravel depending on wave climate	Major river mouths—Skagit, Nooksack, Nisqually, etc.
Tidal flats/salt marshes (no substantial fluvial sediment input)	• Wide mud and sand beaches; extensive intertidal bars and low-tide terrace • Sand, silt, clay sediment mixtures with dense vegetation	Southern Puget Sound—Lynch Cove, Budd Inlet, Henderson Bay, Eld Inlet
Spits	• Sand or mixed sand and gravel with large backshore area. Fine sediments in lagoon	Eastern Strait of Juan de Fuca—Dungeness Spit, Ediz Hook, Sequim Bay, Port Madison; common throughout Puget Sound
Tombolos	• Sand or mixed sand and gravel; lagoon or marshy area between double spits; large backshore area	San Juan Islands and Strait of Juan de Fuca; common throughout Puget Sound
Cuspate forelands	• Sand or mixed sand and gravel beaches; large backshore enclosing lagoon or marsh	Discovery Bay, west side Whidbey and Camano islands, eastern Clallam County (Sequim Bay), Diamond Point
Dunes	• Sand or mixed sand and gravel beach; backshore with sand dunes behind	Northwest Whidbey Island (Cranberry Lake region); otherwise rare in intracoastal areas of Washington
Neutral	**Erosion resistant bedrock or sedimentary strata. Minimum erosion or deposition: low scarps, minor depositional features (Examples, page 14)**	
	• Residual sediment (gravel, cobbles, and boulders) armoring beach; no backshore • Mixed sand, gravel, and cobbles on foreshore with small backshore area • Small shore platform of bedrock with or without veneer of boulders and cobbles	Protected shores in San Juan County
Erosional	**Large erosional scarps cut into bedrock or unconsolidated sediment by marine processes. Occur in regions of vigorous wave action. (Examples, page 14)**	
Erosional scarps in bedrock	• Wave-cut platform with or without a veneer of residual sediment (gravel, cobbles, and boulders) • Pocket beaches between rocky headlands composed of mixed sand, gravel, and cobbles, with a berm and backshore	Outer Strait of Juan de Fuca, San Juan Islands (exposed shores)
Erosional scarps in unconsolidated sediment	• Residual sediment (gravel, cobbles, and boulders) armoring beach; no backshore • Cobble and rocks in areas of high wave action; no backshore area • Mixed sand, gravel, and cobbles on foreshore with small backshore area	Throughout Puget Sound where glacial material is abundant West side Whidbey Island, eastern Strait of Juan de Fuca (Dungeness–Port Angeles)

Coastal Features

Major Features

It is helpful to have a classification scheme with which to organize the great variety of physical features and coastal landforms that one observes along the shores of Puget Sound. A scheme that has proved useful in geological studies and for coastal management in other parts of the world is presented in Table 5.2. With this scheme, a segment of the coast can be placed into one of three major categories, depending on the predominance of erosion and deposition along it. The features which distinguish among depositional, erosional, and neutral coasts are summarized and locations where good examples of these features can be found in the region are given to aid the reader in making use of the classification scheme.

Table 5.3 below summarizes the distribution of coastal features on a county-by-county basis. These data were obtained from an inventory of coastal resources conducted by the Washington State Department of Ecology. Under the heading of modified coasts are included the shores that have been developed for commercial or other purposes and have structures (seawalls, piers, log booms, etc.) on them.

Table 5.3 Distribution of coastal features on a county-by-county basis.

Region	County	Depositional	Neutral	Erosional	Modified
Western	Clallam	80	19	87	34
	Jefferson	92	14	117	46
	Mason	34	3	112	67
	Thurston	118	5	33	43
	Total	324	41	349	190
		11%	**1%**	**11%**	**6%**
Central	Snohomish	80	4	12	54
	King	22	10	35	108
	Kitsap	124	<1	142	114
	Pierce	106	15	105	134
	Total	332	29	294	410
		11%	**1%**	**10%**	**13%**
Northern	Whatcom	22	31	50	38
	Skagit	176	22	67	51
	San Juan	78	95	136	3
	Island	148	22	91	48
	Total	424	170	344	140
		14%	**6%**	**11%**	**5%**
Combined total		**36%**	**8%**	**32%**	**24%**

Minor Features

The shifting sand and gravel deposits on the shore produce a variety of minor sedimentary features that are found on Puget Sound beaches. These include wavy rhythmic features called cusps and linear features called longshore or oblique bars (Fig. 5.4). The photograph of the low-tide terrace at Semiahmoo Spit shows two systems of oblique bars; each one results from a dominant direction of sand movement and wave attack on the spit. The presence of bars and cusps on a beach usually indicates adequate nourishment of the shore with sediment, that is, sufficient sand and gravel for the formation of these features. At some locations, these features remain immobile for several years, moving only during severe storms.

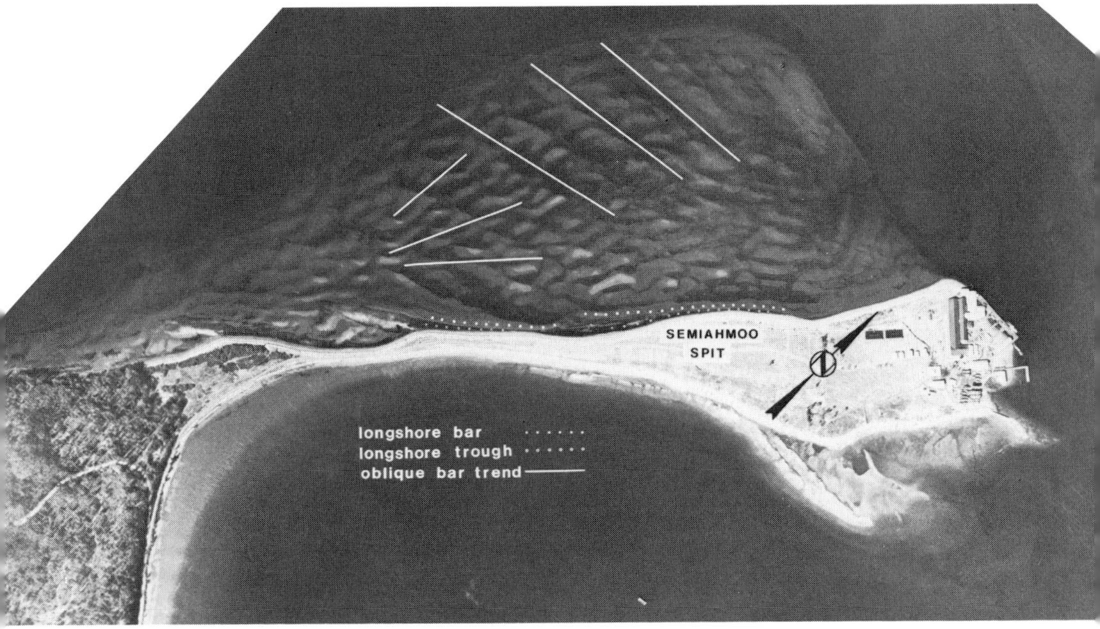

Figure 5.4a Sandbars on the low-tide terrace of Semiahmoo Spit, Whatcom County. Longshore bars parallel the shoreline; oblique bars form at an angle to it. Waves from two dominant directions formed bars at this site. (Photo courtesy Corps of Engineers)

Figure 5.4b Cusps on a gravel beach, Deception Pass State Park.

Figure 5.4c Rill marks produced by water draining from a beach during an ebbing tide, Strait of Juan de Fuca, Clallam County.

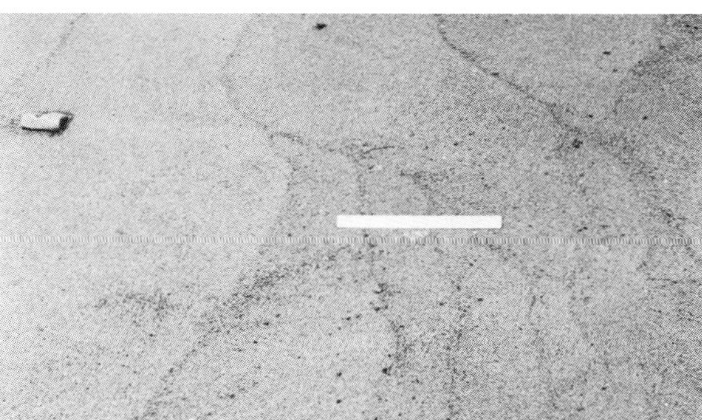

Figure 5.4d Swash marks composed of debris stranded on a beach by receding waves.

Figure 5.4e Ripples produced by tidal currents flowing from left to right over a sandy tidal flat. The downstream sides of current ripples are steeper than the upstream sides.

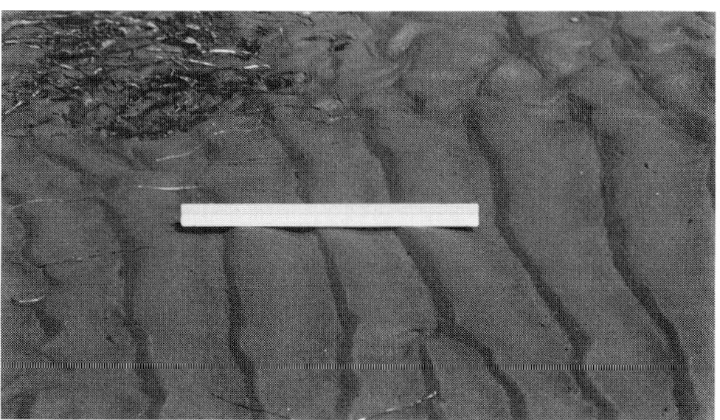

Figure 5.4f Symmetrical ripples formed by waves.

CHAPTER 6

Wave Climate

Waves have a great influence on the oceanographic conditions which shape sedimentary deposits along the exposed shores of Puget Sound. Accurate information about waves not only is an essential part of sensible coastal resource management but contributes to an understanding of the geologic history of the coastal zone as well. Wave effects at a coastal site can be assessed only if the water depth, the wave heights, periods, and frequency of occurrence as well as the directions of wave approach to the coast are known. These wave properties constitute the wave climate at a location. Unlike meteorological climate, which is rather consistent throughout the Puget Sound region, wave climate varies quite radically from place to place because of the varied shape of the coast and uplands, fetch length, water depth, and seasonal changes in wind direction.

Since refraction and diffraction effects must be considered when predicting wave conditions, a detailed description of wave climate on a site-by-site basis is beyond the scope of this volume. Instead, major wave generation areas are distinguished on the basis of prevailing wind conditions and fetch characteristics, and the deep-water waves likely to occur during storms as well as calm periods at selected sites are given based on the limited available data.

Wind Patterns

Wave climate in Puget Sound is linked directly to the seasonal wind patterns of the Pacific Northwest. The general flow of air over western Washington is from the west most of the year. Weather systems acquire moisture and moderate temperature over the North Pacific and move into the Puget Sound region with the prevailing westerly winds. The Olympic Mountains and the Cascade Range channel these winds over the south and central areas of Puget Sound where they blow largely north–south (Fig. 6.1). These prevailing wind directions are parallel with the major channels, basins, passages, and inlets in the Sound. Winds in the Strait of Juan de Fuca are similarly confined by the gap between the Olympic Peninsula and Vancouver Island, and blow predominantly east–west.

During the winter, marine air enters the Puget lowland through Chehalis gap south of the Olympic Peninsula and produces southerly winds over most of lower Puget Sound. The gap between the Cascade

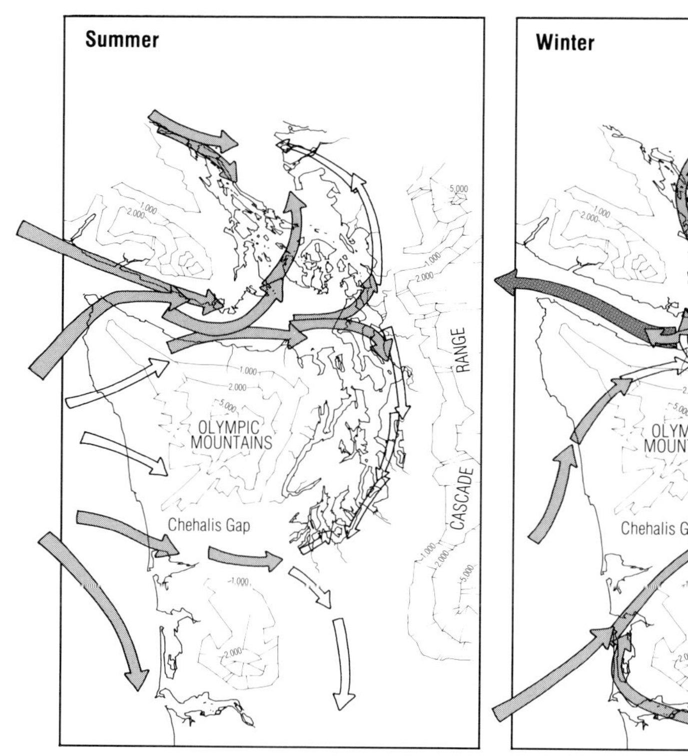

Figure 6.1 Seasonal patterns of the winds over western Washington. Land topography is the dominant influence on wind speed and direction over Puget Sound.

and Olympic ranges closes slightly and causes the air flow to accelerate as it moves north, producing higher wind speeds over the northern waterways than over the lower Sound. For example, wind speeds exceed 8 meters per second (16 knots) more than ten days per month at Whidbey Island compared to five days per month at Olympia. Wind speeds also tend to be faster on the east side than on the west side of the Sound. Winter winds are easterly over the Strait of Juan de Fuca from Cape Flattery to Port Angeles and westerly from Whidbey Island to Dungeness Spit. A circular wind pattern dominates the San Juan Islands and the adjacent coastal areas from Fidalgo Island to Drayton Harbor. This pattern consists of southerly winds to the east of the Islands and northerly winds over Haro Strait to the west.

The regional winds veer to northwesterlies during the spring and continue to blow from the northwest most of the summer. Summer westerlies in the Strait of Juan de Fuca are brisk. They penetrate to Whidbey Island and freshen during the day as solar radiation on the interior landmass heats the air and raises pressure gradients between the cool ocean and warm land. During prolonged warm weather, westerly thermal winds can blow continuously through the night. At Port Angeles, westerlies over 8 meters per second (16 knots) occur 18, 21, and 15 days per month during June, July, and August respectively. At Whidbey Island, the westerlies diverge; weak southerly winds prevail from Padilla Bay to Drayton Harbor and gentle northerly breezes develop over Puget Sound from Admiralty Inlet to Olympia. At Olympia the northerly breezes converge with the onshore flow through the Chehalis gap, resulting in very light surface winds over the lower Sound. With the exception of the Strait of Juan de Fuca, summer wind speeds exceed 8 meters per second (16 knots) only about four days per month in the Puget Sound lowland.

Storms

Storms which bring extreme wind conditions to the Puget Sound region accompany both high and low pressure systems. Low pressure systems are the more common and bring the familiar periods of cool, rainy weather to the area. Extratropical cyclones develop around deep low-pressure systems which occur in the central North Pacific. These storms usually follow a northeasterly track toward the Pacific Northwest coast where they push inland over Vancouver Island. Major cyclones not only generate intense wave activity, but also cause the sea level to rise due to depressed atmospheric pressure and the onshore flow of surface water driven by the wind. It is the combination of large waves with elevated sea level that makes the cyclone so destructive.

Severe cyclones that pass through the region have a wind pattern similar to the one illustrated in Figure 6.2. The frequency and intensity of cyclones are greatest during the winter but moderately high waves can be produced by extratropical cyclones any time from October through May. The most hazardous times are in December and January, however, when the highest tides of the year occur.

Late in the evening of February 12, 1979, a deep, low-pressure system moved ashore across the west end of Vancouver Island and produced very high surface winds over the western half of Washington for more than 12 hours. The storm track over the region is shown in Figure 6.2 and the wind speeds at several reporting stations during the storm are represented by vectors. The numbers on the vectors indicate the position of the storm at the time the winds were observed. This storm remained in positions 4 and 5 over Vancouver Island for about twelve

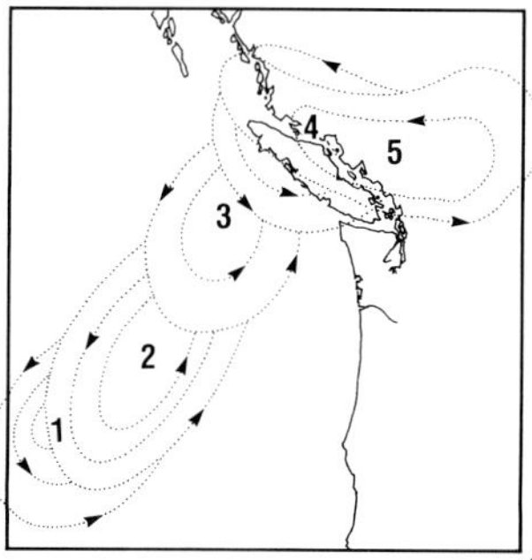

Position of storm	Time
1	Noon/Feb. 12
2	6 p.m./Feb. 12
3	Midnight/Feb. 12
4	6 a.m./Feb. 13
5	Noon/Feb. 13

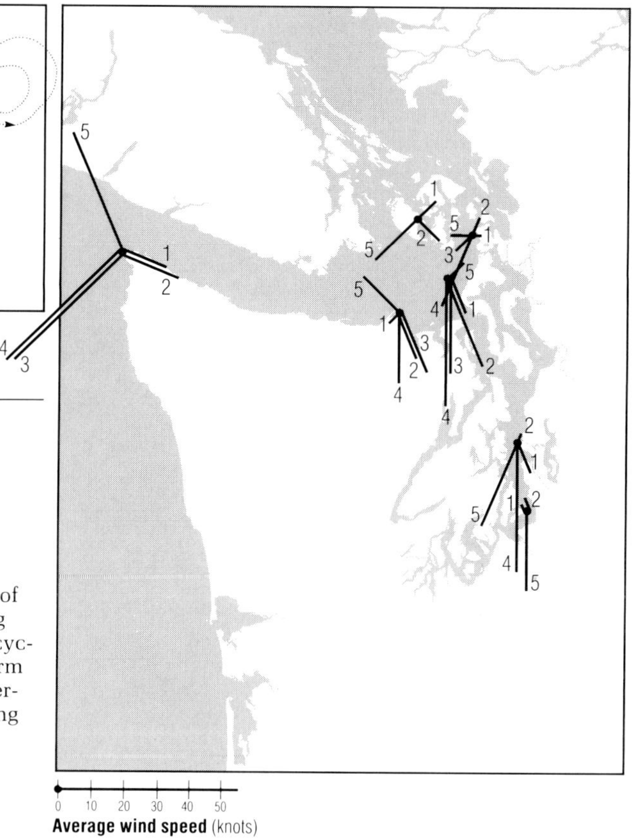

0 10 20 30 40 50
Average wind speed (knots)

Figure 6.2 Development of destructive winds during the severe extratropical cyclone of 1979. Above: Storm positions at six-hour intervals. Right: Corresponding wind speeds at seven coastal sites.

Figure 6.3 Damage to COE experimental erosion control structures at Forbes Point, Whidbey Island caused by the 1979 storm. Lower left: Revetment of gabion mats which failed because backfill was washed out by waves. Right: Log-and-post seawall which failed because backfill washed out leaving facing logs vulnerable to wave and drift log impacts.

hours, and southerly winds averaging 20 meters per second (40 knots) for one- to two-minute periods were prevalent in the central Sound.

Winds at Smith Island and West Point in Seattle averaged 20 meters per second for 6 hours. At Tatoosh Island northwesterlies averaging 20 meters per second blew until noon on the 13th. Large, locally generated waves and ocean swell attacked shores exposed to the northwest from Clallam Bay to Cape Flattery. Little damage was done by these waves, however, because the tide was only half in at the time, causing the waves to break on the lower beach face. Strong southerly winds created high waves which battered most exposed south facing beaches in the central Sound. At the southern tip of San Juan Island, waves calculated from wind speed, duration, and fetch had a significant height of 2.4 meters (8 feet). Maximum wave heights may have exceeded 4.1 meters (13.4 feet). The Hood Canal bridge was destroyed by waves and 40–60 knot winds likely to occur only once per century. Although high winds from 13 to 20 meters per second (26 to 40 knots) from this storm were very persistent at many locations, the major damage to shore property and beaches occurred during a brief period early on the morning of the 13th when strong winds and large waves coincided with an abnormally high tide. During this period, the measured water level at Forbes Point, Whidbey Island was .55 meters (1.81 feet) above the predicted tide; and many of the shore protection structures under evaluation by the COE sustained heavy damage (Fig. 6.3).

A less common but very destructive type of storm occurs when very cold high-pressure air masses spill over the Cascade Range from the continental interior, settle into the Puget lowlands, and produce strong northerly winds over the region. In addition to the regional reversal in wind direction, the wind fields associated with winter high-pressure systems are distinguished from cyclonic storms by two other features. First, the surface winds tend to blow obliquely across the major waterways, rather than paralleling them as do the prevailing winds from cyclones. Also, the duration of high winds over the region is longer since high-pressure centers settle in the lowlands rather than moving east in prevailing westerlies and dissipating as do cyclones.

A particularly energetic storm of this type occurred in January 1951 (Fig. 6.4) when northwesterly winds at Bellingham exceeded 13 meters per second (26 knots) for 46 hours and 18 meters per second (36 knots) for 27 hours. Whereas large wind waves produced by a cyclonic storm are likely to persist only for a single high tide cycle per storm, stationary high-pressure systems can produce extreme wave activity during as many as four consecutive high tides. The potential devastation by high-pressure storms is mitigated somewhat by the regional sea level depression they cause, by elevated atmospheric pressure on the sea surface, and the offshore movement of wind-driven surface water.

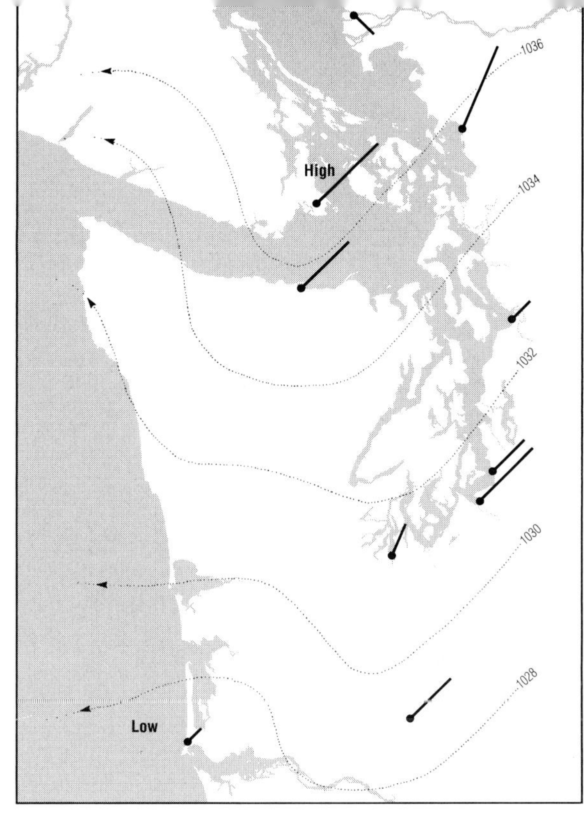

Figure 6.4 High wind speeds during the northerly storm of January 1951 which caused extensive beach erosion and coastal flooding in northern Puget Sound.

0 10 20 30 40 50
Average wind speed (knots)

Wave Generation Areas and Their Wave Spectra

The Strait of Juan de Fuca and the Strait of Georgia are the two largest intracoastal wave generation areas. Both of these waterways are deep and relatively unobstructed by islands. The Strait of Juan de Fuca stretches 115 kilometers (63 nautical miles) from Cape Flattery to Dungeness Spit. It is a restricted seaway only 19.2 kilometers (10.5 nautical miles) wide, however, and the area over which the wind can blow and generate waves is reduced. For this reason the Strait has the fetch characteristics of an open unrestricted body of water only 55 kilometers (30 nautical miles) long. The open water and surrounding terrain of the Strait of Georgia are quite similar to those of the Strait of Juan de Fuca and waves generated by equivalent wind speeds are comparable. Because of these similarities, the wave climates of these straits are considered together.

The frequency of high wave activity drops substantially in the summer and the wave height per storm is lower as well (p. 50). Most of the energy in the sea during calm periods in the Strait of Georgia results from waves with periods of 4 seconds or less. These waves are the short steep variety observed when the wind has recently started to blow; seamen call them "wind chop." Wind chop consists of waves with many different heights and periods. Its spectrum consequently resembles a picket fence and a dominant wave period is less obvious than during a well-developed storm. This is why the energy spectrum for the early period of storm development at Victoria Harbor (p. 36) appears so ragged.

On the basis of the Canadian data for the Strait of Georgia, a reasonable maximum wave height to expect during winter storms with winds of 20 meters per second (40 knots) sustained for several hours is 4.5 meters (14.8 feet). This wave could not travel very far up on a beach, however, because it would break in water about 6.0 meters (20 feet) deep. A wave of this size releases a tremendous amount of energy against rigid structures in deep water, however, and the energy release would be instantaneous rather than gradual as on a gently sloped beach face. Structures fixed or moored in deep water are thus susceptible to the greatest damage from large storm waves. For example, 3.7-meter (12 foot) breakers have plucked armor rocks weighing more than 4 tons off the breakwater at Neah Bay. The base of the breakwater is in about 8.0 meters (30.0 feet) of water and thus very little wave energy is dissipated by shoaling prior to wave impact against the structure.

Only a small fraction of the huge amount of wave energy produced offshore actually arrives at the beaches along the Strait of Juan de Fuca. Many of the larger ocean waves are refracted onto La Perouse and Swiftsure banks at the entrance to the Strait where some of their energy is lost in breaking at sea. Open-ocean wave energy enters the Strait through a small opening in the coast only 19.2 kilometers (10.5 nautical miles) wide and is spread by refraction in shallow water along more than 240 kilometers (130 nautical miles) of coast. Gradual spreading of the wave energy along the coast greatly reduces the wave heights at the beach. Even at Neah Bay where large ocean waves are expected because of its proximity to the open ocean, breaker heights are much smaller than at the exposed beaches of Cape Flattery just 9 kilometers (5 nautical miles) to the west. Refraction at the Neah Bay breakwater can reduce ocean waves from 6.1-meter (20-foot) to 3.5-meter (10.8-foot) breakers, for example (p. 91).

Spits and bay mouth bars are the best indicators of long-term trends in wave direction, since they grow in the direction of net longshore sediment movement. From Cape Flattery to Dungeness, spit and bay mouth bar orientation consistently tend toward the east. Waves from the west apparently have dominated the nearshore current and sediment transport processes along this section of the coast for many hundreds or even thousands of years.

Two dominant wave directions are indicated by spit orientations along the coast from Point Roberts to Lummi Island. The southern half of this shore is exposed to the waves generated by northwesterly winds on the Strait of Georgia; Sandy Point was built by these waves. Semiahmoo and Birch bays, however, receive relatively little wave energy from the Strait of Georgia since they are sheltered by Point Roberts. Semiahmoo Spit and smaller spits in Birch Bay—Terrell Creek Spit, for example—indicate that wave attack is predominantly from the south through southwest. Storm waves at these locations will be about 75 percent of the height of those from the northwest at Sandy Point (Fig. 6.5) because the open water to the south of Semiahmoo Bay is less extensive than in the Strait of Georgia.

The large open waterway surrounding Smith Island is at the junction of three straits, Juan de Fuca, Haro, and Rosario, and Admiralty Inlet and is exposed to winds from most directions. It is unique because, unlike other wave generation areas in the Puget Sound region, it is unrestricted. Unfortunately, no open water wave measurements have been made here, so little is known about their characteristics. Victoria Harbor, Mackaye Harbor, Burrows Bay, Outer Port Discovery, and Dungeness Bay are all exposed to the Smith Island fetch and have similar wave conditions. Waves during calm weather will contain the broad bands of energy at the shorter wave periods typical of conditions measured in the Strait of Georgia (Fig. 6.5). Ocean swells break on the shores with western exposures such as Dungeness Spit and Whidbey Island from Admiralty Head to Deception Pass. Swell waves are not usually destructive, however, since their energy is reduced by refraction. Storms generate seas in the Smith Island fetch with only about 15 percent of the energy characteristic of storm waves generated in the Straits of Georgia and Juan de Fuca.

The Smith Island fetch is located at the junction of several depressions in the surrounding terrain which funnel the wind; these include major river valleys in addition to the waterways mentioned above. From the general pattern of storm and prevailing wind directions, it is clear that waves from several directions have dominated sedimentation on the coast surrounding the Smith Island fetch in recent geologic time, perhaps for the last 5,000 to 7,000 years. The shores around its northern rim are rocky from Deception Pass to San Juan Island and have few beaches of fine material that reveal the predominant sediment transport and wave direction. The southern shores of this region, however, show evidence of long-term wave attack from the northwest and northeast directions. The intensity and duration of wave attack from these directions appear to have been evenly distributed. Consequently, spits of about equal size have developed off the west and east ends of Protection Island and in the mouth of Sequim Bay (Gibson Spit and Kiapot Point). Also Graveyard Spit, a major south-trending feature, has formed within Dungeness Bay, which indicates significant wave attack from the northeast.

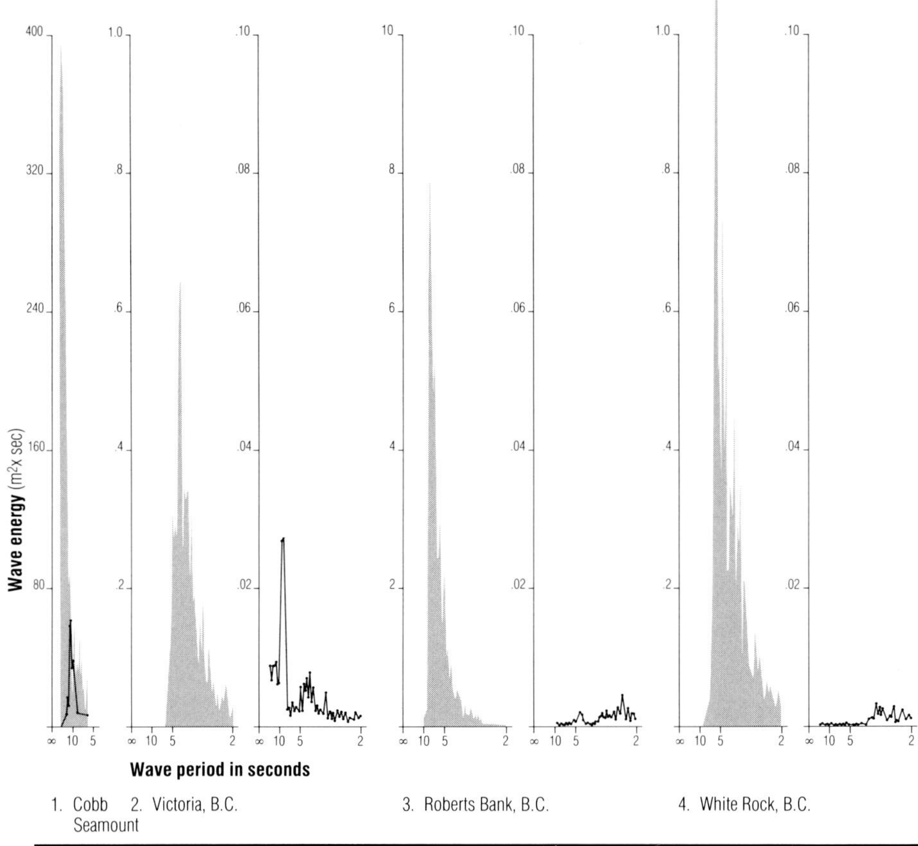

The main basins of Puget Sound from Point Robinson to Admiralty Head, Saratoga Passage, and Port Susan are all relatively restricted fetches with length-to-width ratios ranging from 6:1 to 9:1. Although wind directions generally are parallel to these waterways, large waves rarely develop on them.

Wave energy in sheltered bays and harbors is diminished drastically from the levels in the more open areas such as the Straits of Juan de Fuca and Georgia. The wave spectra for Friday Harbor and Elliott Bay shown on Figure 6.5 are representative of wave conditions in sheltered waters during light to moderate winds. Friday Harbor is exposed to San Juan Channel through narrow channels at both ends of Brown Island and very little wave energy penetrates the harbor from nearby waterways. In Friday Harbor the spectrum represents waves generated by southerly winds. San Juan Island shelters the harbor from southerly winds and this spectrum is typical of calm wave conditions at other

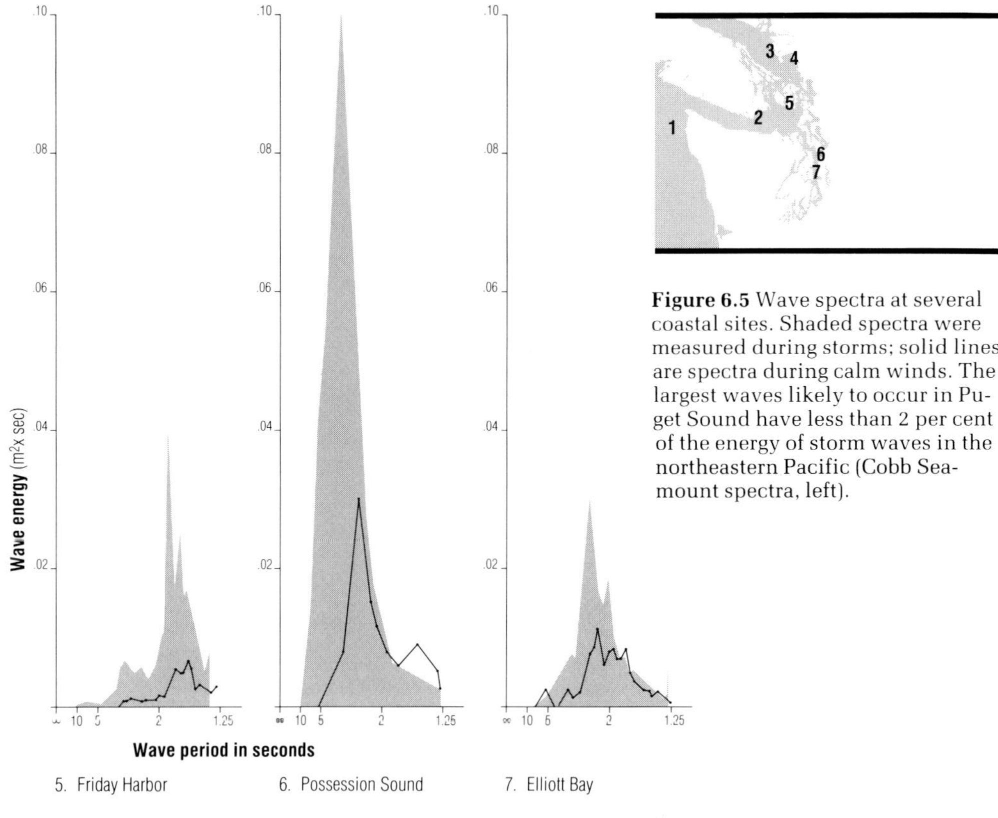

Figure 6.5 Wave spectra at several coastal sites. Shaded spectra were measured during storms; solid lines are spectra during calm winds. The largest waves likely to occur in Puget Sound have less than 2 per cent of the energy of storm waves in the northeastern Pacific (Cobb Seamount spectra, left).

sites in the region. The wave energy level is about the same as the levels during calm periods at Semiahmoo Bay, the Strait of Georgia, and Elliott Bay. The peak wave period is considerably shorter, however, than at other sites and results from the nearly complete isolation of Friday Harbor from longer period waves that might enter from more exposed adjacent waterways.

The Friday Harbor spectrum a characterizes waves generated by moderate winds of 10 meters per second (20 knots) blowing parallel with the length of the harbor (less 1.0 kilometer). Waves under these wind conditions have periods of about 2.0 seconds; and there is a two-fold increase in significant wave height and a three-fold increase in wave energy. Wave data collected at Elliott Bay also characterize waves generated by low wind speeds. Since Elliott Bay is more exposed to open water and has a longer fetch than Friday Harbor, wave lengths and periods are typically longer, 2–2.5 seconds compared to 1.5–2.0 seconds.

Sheltered waterways are the preferred locations for small vessel traffic routes and moorage facilities. Although the wind wave climate may not be destructive to the shoreline in these confined and sheltered areas, vessel wakes can be a major problem. The shores of other commercial port facilities such as Port Angeles, Commencement Bay, Sinclair Inlet, and Fidalgo Bay are exposed to the damaging effects of vessel wakes. The unprotected banks of the Swinomish Slough are particularly susceptible to damage from wakes at high tide.

Little if any wave height data are available for lower Puget Sound. The predominant direction of wave attack, however, is clearly indicated by the orientation of spits in the larger inlets. In Carr Inlet, spits at Fox Island, Horsehead Bay, Huge Creek, and Glen Cove are oriented in a northerly direction. Spits have similar orientations in Case Inlet at Whiteman Cove, Dutchers Bay, Vaughn Bay (p. 10), Dougall Point, and Herron Island. These features indicate that southerly winds are strongest and that the winter wave climate dominates the longshore sediment transport in the area. Most fetches in the southwest portions of the Sound are quite restricted in width; also the wind speeds, particularly in the vicinity of Olympia, are lower than in the northern Sound throughout the year. The combination of these effects produces a low energy wave climate in the southern Sound.

CHAPTER 7

Coastal Hazards

Glaciation in the Puget lowland and subsequent wave and current erosion have created coastal landforms which are unstable. Exposed cliff faces are apt to fail where undercut by waves and saturated with groundwater. Areas which are prone to slope failure are geologically hazardous; low areas have other soil-related problems and are periodically flooded. Consequently, people now using the coastal zone or contemplating its future use should be able to recognize the hazards that may exist and how to contend with them.

Hazards of Coastal Cliffs

Landslides

The movements of soils and rock materials on steep coastal terrain common in this region include landslides, rockfalls, and earthflows. Landslides and earthflows occur in surface soils and glacial deposits and are prevalent natural features of the shoreline throughout Puget Sound. Figure 7.1 shows a major slide in the face of a 90-meter (300-foot) bluff composed of Vashon Till and unconsolidated sand and gravel. In a recent inventory of eleven counties in the Puget Sound region (excluding Clallam County) nearly 33 percent of the shoreline appeared unstable and more than 700 coastal sites with active landslides or evidence of past landslides were identified (Table 7.1). In the central Puget Sound area, Alki and Picnic points, Redondo Beach, Perkins Lane, and Duwamish Head are sites where slope stability problems have become critical in recent years because of increased development. Since groundwater and surface runoff are contributing factors to these problems, most landslides coincide with heavy precipitation and ground freezing during winter and early spring.

A landslide begins along a zone of weakness in slope material when its weight exceeds the frictional resistance holding it in place. The steeper a slope, the more likely slippage will occur. Figure 7.2 shows fifty slides categorized by their associated ground slope angles. Increases of more than 20 percent in the cumulative percentage of landslides occur at slope angles of approximately 15 and 25 degrees. These data indicate that slides in glacial material characteristic of the Seattle area are infrequent on slopes less than about 15 degrees but be-

Figure 7.1 Large landslide of glacial sediment, mostly sand and gravel, at Possession Beach, Whidbey Island. (Photo courtesy D. Frank, USGS)

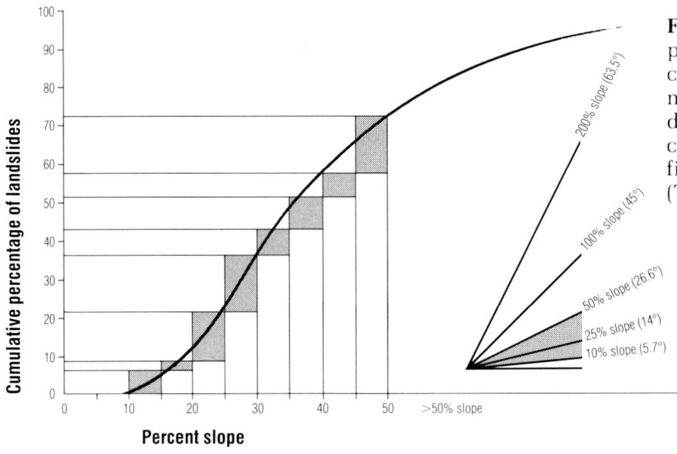

Figure 7.2 Increase of the probability of landslide occurrence with slope steepness. Shaded rectangles indicate the incremental change of probability per five percent of slope (Tubbs, 1974 data).

County	Unstable upland slopes (miles)	Percentage of shoreline	Number of recent or old landslides
Clallam (no data)			
Island	112.0	5.7%	15
Jefferson	81.0	4.2%	315
King	66.0	3.3%	62
Kitsap	50.0	2.6%	94
Mason	96.0	4.9%	65
Pierce	72.0	3.7%	76
San Juan	13.0	0.7%	16
Skagit	46	2.4%	21
Snohomish	19.0	0.9%	19
Thurston	50.0	2.6%	12
Whatcom	35.5	1.8%	23
Total	640.5	32.8%	718

Table 7.1 Slope stability and landslide statistics summarized by county (Washington DOE data).

come very likely on slopes steeper than 25 degrees. Visible signs of slide activity other than slope angle are debris accumulations at the base of a slope, barren scars in the cliff face, leaning trees, and cracks in the soil near the cliff edge.

Visible signs provide superficial evidence of the risk of a slide. Of greater importance to slide forecasting are the physical properties of the material forming the slopes. Since these properties are difficult and costly to determine prior to a slide, most information on slope failures has been acquired when the slope materials are exposed after sliding. Mechanical weaknesses in slopes are usually associated with bedding surfaces and fault planes in rock strata, as well as boundaries between materials of contrasting water permeability. Resistance to sliding along these surfaces is attributed to many complex and interrelated factors. Hydrostatic pressure is the major factor in glacial sediments of this region, and rainwater percolation through the ground raises this pressure and the likelihood of slide occurrence.

Most slides in the Seattle area involve glacial sediments in the stratigraphic section shown in Figure 1.3 (p. 3). The Vashon Till at the top of the section is a mixture of sediments from clay to boulders, compacted by the weight of glacial ice, and is relatively impermeable to water. The underlying advance outwash and Esperance Sand are more uniformly sized materials through which groundwater percolates freely. In contrast, the Lawton Clay is a fine-grained sediment, largely silt and clay, that has very low permeability. Major portions of this section are exposed in coastal bluffs throughout Puget Sound. Many bluffs consisting of these materials are very unstable and a rapid influx of groundwater can easily trigger sliding.

In most years, Puget Sound receives moderate precipitation, usually as rain and at a rather steady rate. The northern and central areas receive about 90 centimeters (35 inches) and the southern areas receive about 120 centimeters (50 inches) annually. Some areas of Clallam and San Juan counties are in the rain shadow of the Olympic Mountains and receive only about 43 centimeters (17 inches) per year of precipitation. Average monthly precipitation is greatest from October through February (Fig. 7.3).

Beginning in mid fall, groundwater percolation through the permeable sand layers in coastal bluffs increases, raising the water table slightly. Groundwater does not penetrate into the silt and clay beds, but flows through the sand layers on top of them until it drains from the face of the bluff. As long as the rate of water infiltration is balanced by drainage from the sand layers, hydrostatic pressures within the sand layer remain low and slope stability is unaffected. When drainage is blocked or infiltration increases rapidly, excessive water pressures build up in the sand. The hydrostatic pressure and added weight of the water, as well as its lubricating effects between the sand and clay layers, cause the sand layer to yield to gravity and slide. Conditions that are effectively the reverse of the above situation also cause slides. That is, hydrostatic pressure in a sand layer builds up beneath clay-rich impermeable material and causes the impermeable material to slide. The latter situation is much less common than the former.

The frequency of landslides in unconsolidated material, with other factors held constant, is most closely correlated with the supply of groundwater by rainfall (Fig. 7.4). Figure 7.4 summarizes data documenting Seattle landslides of 1971–1972, a period when several storms brought intense short-term rainfall to the area. It can be seen that landslides are five times more likely when heavy rainfall occurs in one day than when the same amount of rain falls in a 2- to 5-day period.

When geological and environmental factors combine to produce unstable slopes, slides can be initiated more easily by earthquakes and human activity. Puget Sound is located in a zone of relatively high seismic activity and has been affected by at least seven large earthquakes in modern times. The 1949 earthquake is the largest to have occurred in the region. It had a magnitude of 7.1 on the Richter scale and its epicenter was located between Tacoma and Olympia. An earthquake of this magnitude is statistically unlikely to occur more than once in 160 years. Aside from the direct effects of this large earthquake on structures, ground motion from the 1949 earthquake triggered a large slide at Salmon Beach on the Tacoma Narrows. This slide occurred along 400 meters (1,450 feet) of shore bluff and involved more than one million cubic yards of glacial material. A slide of this size could be devastating if it occurred near a beach community located below a bluff.

Also of concern with major seismically triggered slides are the waves that are generated when the material plunges into nearshore waters. According to local residents, the Possession Beach slide (Fig. 7.1) generated a "twelve-foot wave" that damaged boats, homes, and foundations in the nearby area. Were a similar volume of material to slide into a deep semi-enclosed bay, a common feature in Puget Sound, wave damage to adjacent beach communities could be substantial. Fortunately, major slides are relatively rare; and month-to-month seismic activity is so low that it is not correlated with the observed monthly frequency of landsliding (Fig. 7.3).

Other kinds of slope failure occur in the local glacial deposits. In Skagit and Whatcom counties, for example, shore bluffs composed of clay-rich glaciomarine drift are prone to sliding. This material, consolidated when dry, loses cohesion and shear strength when saturated with water and slumps onto the beach, leaving characteristic bowl-shaped scars in the bluff face. The west and southwest facing shores at Birch Bay and from Neptune Beach to Whitehorn Point, as well as several

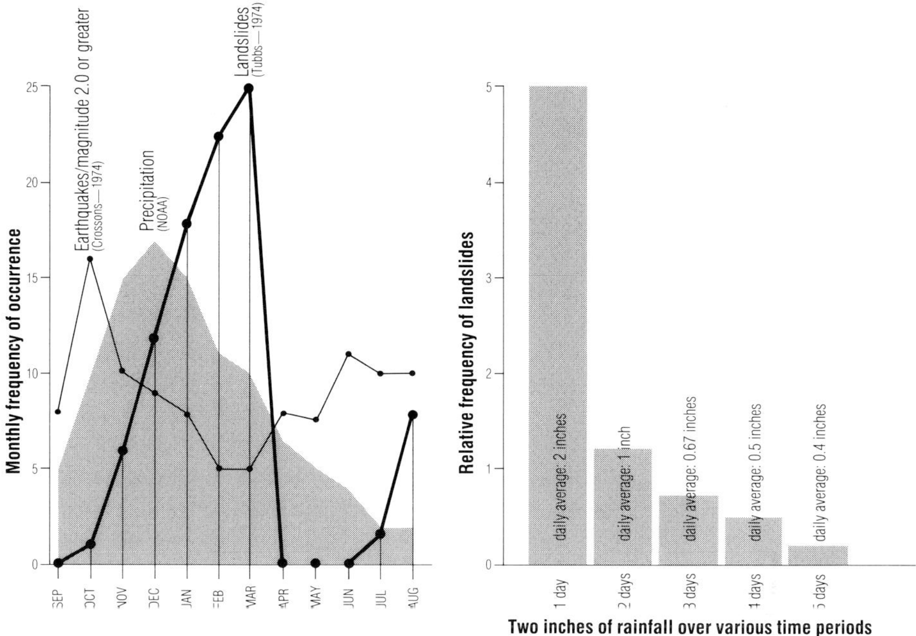

Figure 7.3 Annual trends of precipitation and occurrence of landslides and earthquakes. The peak in landslide frequency is best correlated with peak precipitation but lags it by three months.

Figure 7.4 Landslide frequency versus daily average rainfall (Tubbs, 1974 data).

sites around Bellingham Bay, are locations where these slides have occurred.

Slides in exposed bedrock usually happen after waves have undercut the cliff foundation. Bedrock slides are prevalent along the shores of Clallam County, west of Agate Bay, where the coastal cliffs are composed of sedimentary rocks of the Twin Rivers Formation. In Skagit and Whatcom counties glacial scouring has steepened many bedrock slopes, creating upland slide hazards. Along Chuckanut Drive, south of Larrabee State Park and at the east side of Chuckanut Bay, rockslides have occurred along fractures and bedding planes that dip at a slightly steeper angle than the slope faces. Similar slides have occurred recently along the southwest shore of Lummi Island and on Ika Island in Skagit Bay.

Rockfalls are distinguished from landslides in that they involve dislodged rock fragments that fall freely or roll down slopes steeper than 50 degrees. Usually they occur suddenly or as an intermittent series of very short events. Figure 7.5 shows a small rockfall near Larrabee Park, Skagit County. Under natural conditions, rockfall can be initiated by excessive precipitation, seismic activity, wave erosion, and multiple freeze-thaw cycles (when ice in cracks wedges the rock loose).

Figure 7.5 Rockfall near Larrabee Park, Skagit County.

Since rockfalls are confined to shores with exposed cliffs of jointed or faulted bedrock, they occur most frequently in the northern part of Puget Sound where these formations are exposed. In Whatcom and Skagit counties, rockfalls are common on Lummi Island, and at the north end of Cypress Island. At some coastal sites in Clallam, Jefferson, and San Juan counties the bluffs are composed of cemented gravels, silts, and clays; and large slabs break off and fall when undercut by wave erosion. This occurs east of the Elwha River and near Green Point, Clallam County and in San Juan County along the western sides of Lopez and Waldron islands.

Earthflows

Earthflows are surface phenomena in which a fluid-like viscous mixture of sediment, debris, and water flows downslope. They are initiated by torrential rainfall (sometimes preceded by frost) which produces a slurry of eroded soil. Earthflows are also possible in dry, noncohesive sand and gravel deposits which rest on steep rocky slopes. Slight disturbances can cause these materials to flow rapidly downslope. Earthflows occur on north facing slopes of Miller Peninsula, Jefferson County and on Pigeon Point, Whatcom County. At the latter location, forest fires destroyed the ground cover and may have enhanced the rapid infiltration of the soil by runoff which caused the slides. Dry earthflows also occur in Quaternary sediments east of Green Point, Jefferson County and along the east and west shores of Lopez Island, San Juan County.

The frequency and severity of slope stability problems are increased by improper construction techniques and land development practices. Of the Seattle landslides, mentioned earlier, at least 40 percent involved man-caused modifications to slopes or environmental factors that contributed to slope failure. In fact, all of the natural factors that lead to slope instability can be duplicated by people in the course of normal development activities. Excessive runoff and infiltration are frequently produced by irrigation, inadequate drainage of paved surfaces, and the removal of trees and ground covering plants from slopes. Sanitary drainfields place additional demands on the internal drainage capacity of coastal bluffs. These practices produce the same hazardous increases in groundwater as periods of intense rainfall. Modifications of natural upland slopes to provide hillside building sites, particularly the removal of material from the toe of a slope, can promote sliding in much the same way that wave erosion does. Finally, the additional weight of fill material placed on unstable slopes may cause them to fail if their load-bearing capacity is exceeded.

Soil Liquefaction and Subsidence

Most shores along sheltered embayments, deltas, and wetlands are underlain with saturated organic-rich soils that are compressible and flow under external stresses. Soil liquefaction occurs when highly porous fine sands and clays collapse and flow sideways in response to increases in external lateral forces. These forces may result from heavy construction, and soil shifting is often triggered by vibrations associated with traffic, industrial, or seismic activity. The onset of soil liquefaction usually accompanies long periods of precipitation, irrigation, and other activities affecting the groundwater level. Once saturated with water, soil with slight agitation behaves like a fluid because most of the external stresses act directly on the pore water rather than on the particles of soil. Liquefied soil will flow on relatively flat ground when it is unevenly loaded. Soil in the liquefied state can flow from underneath and away from building foundations and other structures.

Differential settlement, on the other hand, involves the downward displacement of compressible surface material with little or no horizontal movement. It can result from the compaction of organic materials in the soil or the removal of pore water from the soil structure through wells or springs. In coastal areas of Puget Sound, settlement is most frequently caused by compaction of subsurface organic material and porous clays rather than water removal from soil.

The hazard to developments on water-saturated alluvium or estuarine deposits in low coastal areas is aggravated by their unique response to seismic disturbances. Seismic waves produced by local earthquakes are amplified strongly when they pass through unconsolidated soils overlying bedrock. Amplification of the wave form by a factor of ten is possible (Fig. 7.6); the result is that larger ground motions and higher earthquake intensities are felt in low-lying depositional areas. The best documented instance of extensive ground failure in these modes occurred during the 1965 earthquake in the industrialized

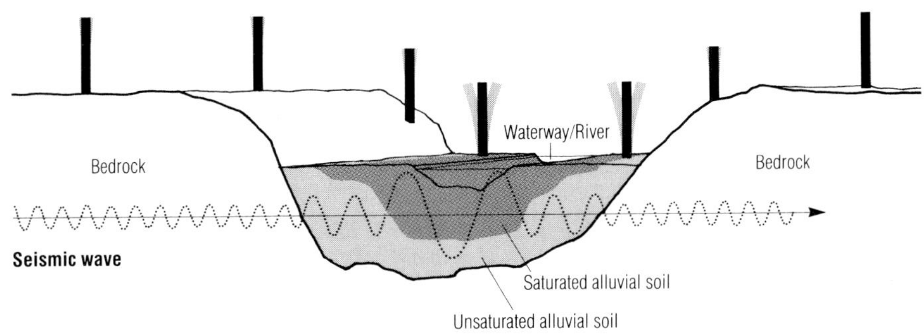

Figure 7.6 Amplification of a seismic wave passing through unconsolidated sediments.

areas near the Duwamish waterway. Most of this area was filled with unconsolidated soils dredged from nearby waterways. Triggered by the earthquake, these soils settled differentially, causing riverside structures to shift laterally with extensive damage to foundations.

Oil on Beaches

There is a special class of hazards for which only people can be held responsible. They result from the release of pollutants into coastal waters. Historically, the major concerns related to coastal pollution have involved the biological resources of the coast, primarily commercial and recreational fisheries. Although these effects are, for the most part, beyond the scope of this book, oil spills must be considered a coastal hazard because pollution of beaches and estuarine shores can drastically alter their physical quality. Major oil spills in the recent past such as those at Santa Barbara, California and along the Brittany Coast of France have focused attention worldwide on some of the physical effects of spills.

The grounding of the *Amoco Cadiz* off the French coast delivered 431,550 barrels (one barrel = 42 gallons) of crude oil to 390 kilometers of beaches and rocky shores. Although damage of this magnitude is unlikely in Puget Sound since the open ocean waves that dispersed the oil so widely are not present in most of the region, very large quantities of oil are transferred over navigable waters to land-based distribution systems on a regular basis. In the period between 1972 and 1974, the quantity of oil transported on Puget Sound and its approaches increased from 45,000 to 105,000 barrels per day. Until now (1982), most of this oil has been brought here to meet regional energy needs, but transshipment facilities and pipelines are now being considered to supply the future oil needs of midwestern states as well. These developments could increase the daily volumes of oil shipments to 1.3 million barrels per day.

Public awareness of the risk of oil spills and the perception of public concern by the petroleum industry has spurred substantial improvement in the technology to handle oil safely. For these and other reasons, Puget Sound residents are indeed fortunate not to have experienced a major oil spill. Nonetheless, with increased frequency and size of oil shipments there is an attendant increase in the risk of a spill.

The primary route of oil tankers entering Puget Sound follows the Strait of Juan de Fuca, passes through Rosario Strait, and continues to the oil refineries at Anacortes and Cherry Point (Fig. 7.7). Based on studies of oil spills in other parts of the world with similar climate and coastal setting, the U.S. Geological Survey has developed a system for ranking coastal features according to their tendency to retain and accumulate spilled oil (Table 7.2). This system assigns a vulnerability number from 1 to 10 to segments of the coast. High vulnerability numbers indicate segments of the coast where oil is likely to accumulate and degrade the shore physically for periods up to a decade. Lower vulnerability numbers indicate shorelines that retain oil for only a few weeks or months.

When crude oil is spilled on coastal waters, natural processes rapidly change it physically and chemically (Fig. 7.8). Initially, the oil spreads out under the influence of gravity to form a thin film. Evaporation of the more volatile low-density components of the oil can account for losses of oil to the atmosphere of up to 20 percent in the first two days after it is spilled. A smaller portion of the oil, depending on the weather, is oxidized by the sun or dissolves in the surface waters. The remaining oil spreads on the surface and is transported by tidal currents, waves, and the wind. In the process of spreading, water is mixed into the oil and if the mixing is vigorous an oily emulsion with the consistency of chocolate mousse is formed. Because this emulsion is largely water, it can have a greater volume than the original spill. In addition to the other losses, some of the denser compounds which do not evaporate easily attach to suspended sediments in the water column and sink to the seabed. The residual floating oil will find its way to shore and accumulate on beaches and tidal mud flats. The volume of stranded oil deposits is determined by a complex interaction of many factors; the major ones include wave climate, sediment porosity, and the slope of the beach surfaces. Horizontal porous sediment surfaces will hold more oil than steep bedrock surfaces.

On beaches, the onshore thrust of breaking waves herds the oil into pools and holds it against the beach. With time the oil pools move up the beach under the influence of the tides and accumulate at the high-tide line. Once removed from the zone of wave action, the oil can percolate into the beach and form asphalt-like mixtures with beach sediments. The depth of oil penetration into the beach sediments depends on the oil viscosity and sediment size. Gravel beaches are more likely to

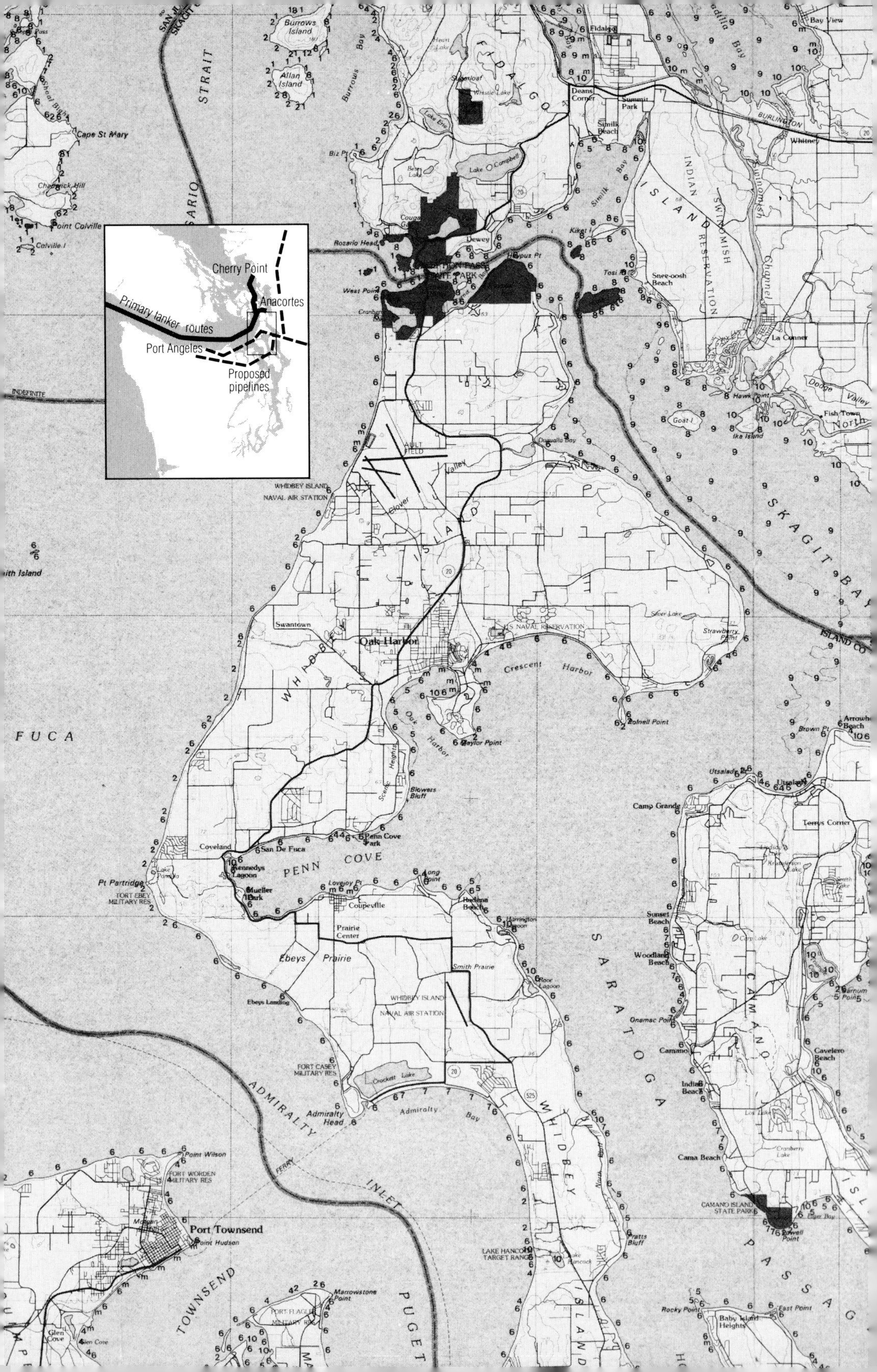

Cherry Point
Anacortes
Primary tanker routes
Port Angeles
Proposed pipelines
Burrows Island
Allan Island
Burrows Bay
Cape St Mary
Point Colville
Colville I
Fidalgo
Deans Corner
Summit Park
Similk Beach
Bay View
Burlington
Whitney
Lake Campbell
Similk Bay
Indian
Island
Reservation
Swinomish
Channel
Rosario Head
West Point
Dewey
Kiket I
Hoypus Pt
Snee-oosh Beach
La Conner
Hawk Point
Goat I
Fish Town
Dodge
Valley
Ika Island
North
Ault Field
Clover
Valley
Whidbey Island Naval Air Station
Skagit Bay
Island Co
Smith Island
Swantown
Oak Harbor
Whidbey
Island
U.S. Naval Reservation
Crescent Harbor
Strawberry Point
Silver Lake
Polnell Point
Fuca
Maylor Point
Oak Harbor
Scenic Heights
Blowers Bluff
Brown Pt
Utsalady
Camp Grande
Terrys Corner
Coveland
San De Fuca
Penn Cove Park
Penn Cove
Kennedys Lagoon
Pt Partridge
Fort Ebey Military Res
Lovejoy Pt
Long Point
Coupeville
Prairie Center
Ebeys Prairie
Smith Prairie
Ebeys Landing
Whidbey Island Naval Air Station
Harrington Lagoon
Saratoga
Sunset Beach
Woodland Beach
Camano
Barnum Point
Onamac Point
Camano
Cavelero Beach
Indian Beach
Fort Casey Military Res
Crockett Lake
Admiralty Head
Admiralty Bay
Admiralty
Inlet
Whidbey
Cama Beach
Cranberry Lake
Camano Island State Park
Lowell Point
Passage
Point Wilson
Fort Worden Military Res
Port Townsend
Point Hudson
Ferry
Puget
Townsend
Lake Hancock Target Range
Lake Hancock
Pratts Bluff
Island
Marrowstone Point
Glen Cove
Rocky Point
Baby Island Heights
East Point

Figure 7.7 Left: Map of oil spill vulnerability for the shores of northern Puget Sound. An explanation of the vulnerability rankings is given in Table 7.2, page 84. Inset: Primary oil-tanker routes.

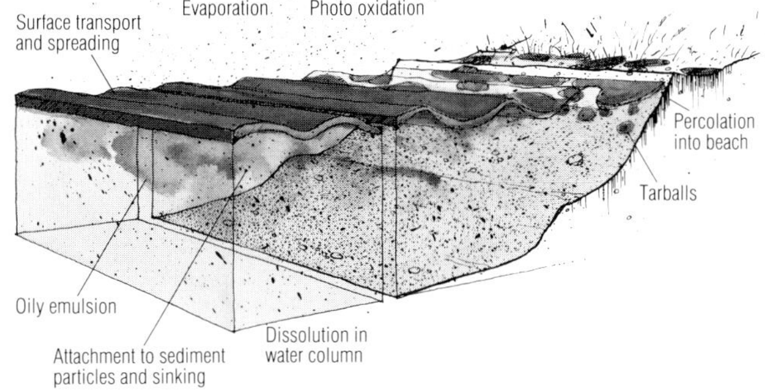

Figure 7.8 Chemical and physical processes that weather spilled crude oil and disperse it in coastal waters and on beaches.

be deeply penetrated by oil than ones composed of fine sand. For example, penetration depths of more than 0.5 meters (1.6 feet) have been observed on gravel and cobble beaches; 10–20-centimeter (4–8 inches) penetrations are likely on mixed sand and gravel beaches. But oil would only percolate into the upper few centimeters of a fine sand beach. In addition to percolation, the oil can be buried during cycles of coastal erosion and deposition. On exposed beaches of the Strait of Juan de Fuca, oil stranded after winter erosion could be buried by as much as one to two meters of sediment during beach rebuilding in the summer months.

Rocky shores are the least vulnerable to long-term accumulations of spilled oil. The principal reasons are that these shores do not have sediment in the intertidal zone that could retain oil and horizontal surfaces for oil to cling to are usually absent. The bedrock cliffs exposed to moderate and high energy waves along the outer Strait of Juan de Fuca and parts of Rosario Strait resist oil because waves reflected from them tend to hold oil slicks several meters offshore. Also, if the base of a bedrock cliff has been wetted by spray from waves, oil does not cling to the rock. In certain areas, wave-cut platforms exist adjacent to rocky shores (p. 14) and oil will accumulate on these platforms, particularly if tide pools and other irregularities exist there.

Tidal flats are the most vulnerable to long-term retention of spilled oil. The severity of the pollution varies somewhat depending on the type of sediments on the intertidal shore. In areas with low to moderate wave energy, the tidal flat is sandy and resists oil percolation into the bed below a few centimeters. Oil stranded on these shores is moved onto the beaches adjacent to the tidal flat by wave and tidal action where percolation and retention is more likely. Muddy tidal flats, however, will retain oil because they exist in areas sheltered from wave activity. Oil retention in these areas is enhanced because clay and silt tend to absorb oil and retain it for periods of several years.Since these shores have salt marshes adjacent to them there is additional risk that oil will accumulate in the intertidal vegetation in the same way that sediment does (Fig. 2.4, p. 19). Major tidal flats adjacent to the oil transport route are located at the Dungeness and Lummi rivers and in Samish, Fidalgo, and Padilla bays. Figure 7.9 illustrates the relative vulnerability to the retention of spilled oil of coastal areas along the major oil transport route.

Unlike the geological and natural hazards discussed earlier with which people must contend as they develop the coastal zone, oil spills are man-caused hazards over which they fortunately have some control and responsibility.

Table 7.2 Vulnerability of coastal features to spilled oil, expressed as residence time of oil, according to U.S. Geological Survey (Figure 7.7) and NOAA Office of Oceanography and Marine Services/Ocean Assessment Division (Figure 7.8) rankings.

Feature	Residence Time of oil	U.S.G.S. ranking	NOAA ranking
Exposed rocky shores	Days to weeks	1	1
Wave-cut platforms	Days to weeks	2	2
Fine-sand beaches	Days to weeks	3	4
Coarse-sand beaches	Months	4	No ranking given
Exposed sandy tidal flats	Months	5	7
Sand and gravel beaches	Years	6	5
Gravel beaches	Years	7	6
Sheltered rocky shores	Years	8	8
Tidal mud flats	Years	9	9
Marshes and lagoons	10 Years	10	10(●)

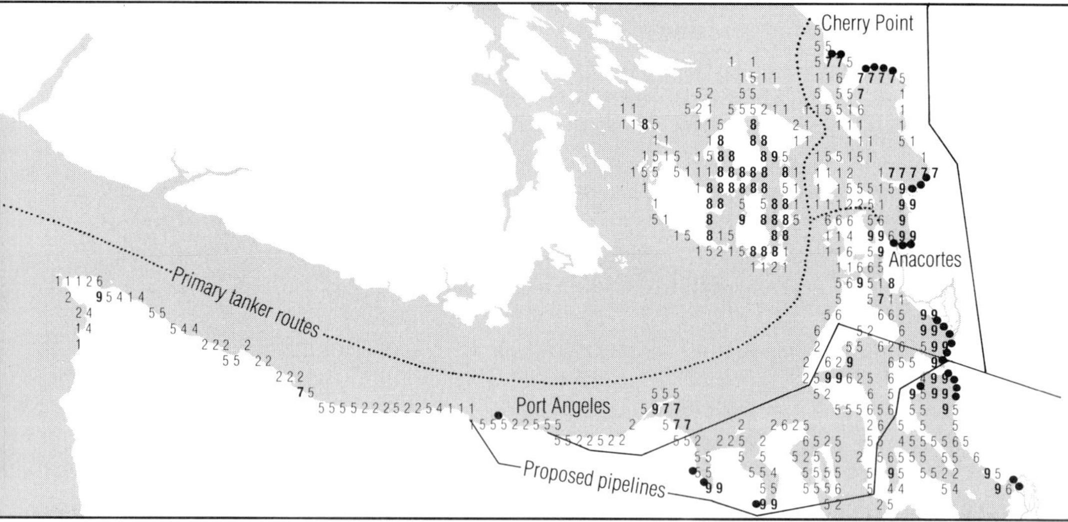

Figure 7.9 Vulnerability of coastal areas along oil transport routes to long-term effects of spilled crude oil. Vulnerability rankings are given in Table 7.2.

CHAPTER 8

Development of the Coast
Progress and Problems

People's early coastal projects on the shores of Puget Sound must have been practical and uncomplicated endeavors designed to solve water access and fishing problems. An archaeological site at Conway, Skagit County contains relics of structures for trapping fish built by Indians 700 years ago on a distributary of the Skagit River. These Native American engineers had to complete only a short checklist before construction could begin. Three of their major design considerations would probably have been to: (1) select a suitable site (there were many to choose from in those days), (2) locate a source of construction material, and (3) design the simplest appropriate structure. The entire process of solving these three engineering problems may have taken a few days to a few weeks.

In this region, as in other heavily developed coastal areas of the United States, the engineering of coastal structures which affect natural processes on a large scale has become very complex. The time necessary for the solution of preconstruction engineering problems for a large coastal structure such as the Shilshole Marina in Seattle or the shore protection structures on Ediz Hook can be as long as seven years. Both design complexities and preparation time have escalated rapidly in the past few decades for a number of reasons. A major one is that the portion of the coast which is undergoing private development has increased dramatically and more elaborate structures are required to utilize a dwindling number of sites, many of which are not very well suited for the planned activity.

Inflationary trends in the costs of materials, labor, and financing have made the cost-to-benefit ratio an essential consideration in all design work. Finally, the public interest in the coastal resources affected by the project must also be considered. Public concern over environmental issues has forced the developer as well as the coastal engineer to consult with knowledgeable experts from other disciplines such as the geological, oceanographical, meteorological, biological, and fisheries sciences during the project design phase. For these reasons, the design of coastal structures has become a truly interdisciplinary decision-making process. It involves the application of sound technology as well as extensive legal and administrative action to get a project proposal through the permit acquisition procedures intended to protect all influenced parties.

Historically, the principal coastal engineering problems have changed in response to the varied trends in development of the Puget Sound region. Late nineteenth century engineers dealt primarily with water access (piers, docks, and canals) and the establishment of coastal transportation lines for forest products and intercity commerce. As ship traffic expanded to meet the demands of growing industries, so did the problems of navigation channel and harbor maintenance. Control of shoaling, flooding, and erosion with structures such as levees and seawalls was a common concern not only to maintain harbors but to protect adjacent uplands.

The Army Corps of Engineers is required by the Rivers and Harbors Act of 1899 to review all plans and designs for developments or improvements on the coast and to issue a permit before construction may begin. In recent years, new trends of coastal development have occurred and some of these are apparent in the statistics on COE permit applications given in Table 8.1. Navigation and shipping-related structures remain at the top of the list as indicated by the large percentage of permits issued for projects involving pilings, buoys, and floats. The second most prevalent activity is filling which is related to the growing shortage of coastal construction sites with grades and slopes suitable for current development needs. Erosion control is the third major coastal engineering problem in Puget Sound and again reflects the pressures caused by the dwindling number of stable, protected coastal sites.

Structure/Activity	Number issued	Percentage of total sampled
Docks, piers, and pilings	249	28%
Dredge and fill	191	22%
Shore protection structures (bulkheads, breakwaters, dikes, groins)	140	16%
Floats and booms	107	13%
Vessel moorage and repair	69	8%
Submarine cables and pipes	26	3%
Outfall and intake structures	23	3%
Buildings	18	2%
Aquaculture	17	2%
Dredge spoils disposal	13	2%
Log dumps	2	less than 1%

Table 8.1 Development and construction activities on coastal areas of Puget Sound during the late 1970s from COE permit data.

In this chapter some current trends in engineering practice and aspects of the siting and construction of coastal structures that are specifically related to the conditions in the Puget Sound region are discussed. The intent is to acquaint owners and future developers of shore property with the basic phases of decision making that go into a sound engineering job and give some examples of well-engineered projects as well as some that were not. It must be emphasized that this chapter is not a guide to engineering procedures nor are the data presented with case studies necessarily applicable to new or future projects. The COE *Shore Protection Manual* is the most generally accepted compendium of coastal engineering procedures now available and is recommended to anyone with a moderate level of technical knowledge.

The Permit

The Shoreline Management Act is intended to promote use of coastal resources that: (1) minimize environmental damage, (2) enhance public access and recreation, (3) encourage water-dependent uses of coastal resources, and (4) preserve a balance between property rights and environmental protection. Water-dependent activities are those which cannot exist except at coastal sites; ferry terminals, aquaculture, and port facilities are examples. The original role of the COE in the permit process was to prevent alteration and obstruction of navigable waters. Since the passage of Federal Water Pollution Control Act amendments and the Clean Water Act in the 1970s, the COE mission has been expanded. It now includes the maintenance of water quality in protected marshes, swamps, and similar valuable wetlands resources.

Many activities and structural improvements that alter the physical condition of the beach, shore, or adjacent uplands require review, approval, or a formal permit from a hierarchy of local, state, and federal agencies. These agencies are charged with the responsibility of protecting the interests of the public at all levels from local to national. For the most part, local governments decide if a project proposal is acceptable; however, approval may be denied at any level in the permit system. Whether or not a permit is required, it is usually most cost efficient and expedient for the property owner to consult with an engineer as well as the technical staff of the appropriate city and county planning and building departments before the design phase. These individuals can make suggestions about the engineering feasibility and legal aspects of the project as well as give guidance on permit requirements.

Table 8.1 lists most of the shoreline improvements and activities that may require a permit. When any of these affect navigation or water quality seaward of the mean high water line, a COE permit application (Engineering Form 4345) must be filed. For COE permits, mean high

Figure 8.1 Steps required to obtain a permit to develop or make improvements to a coastal site. Right: Detail of COE review which occurs concurrently with local government action.

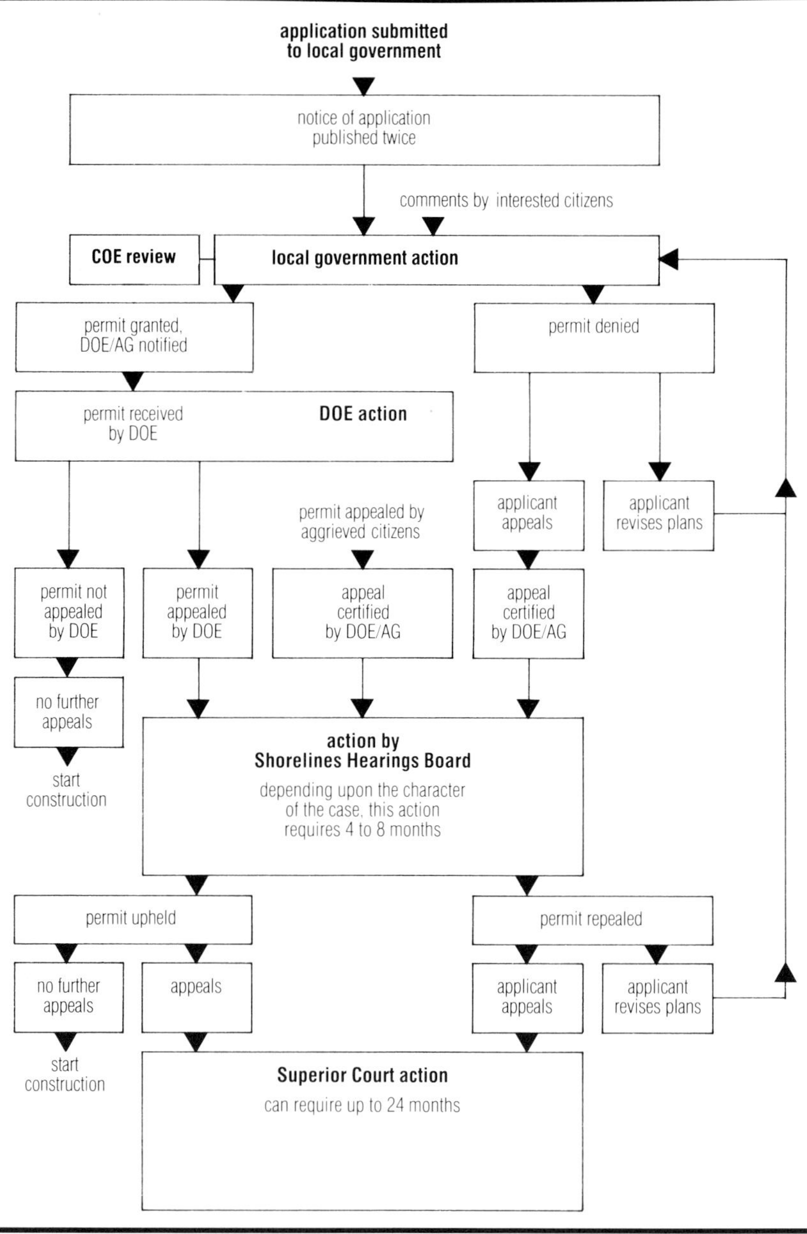

COE Review

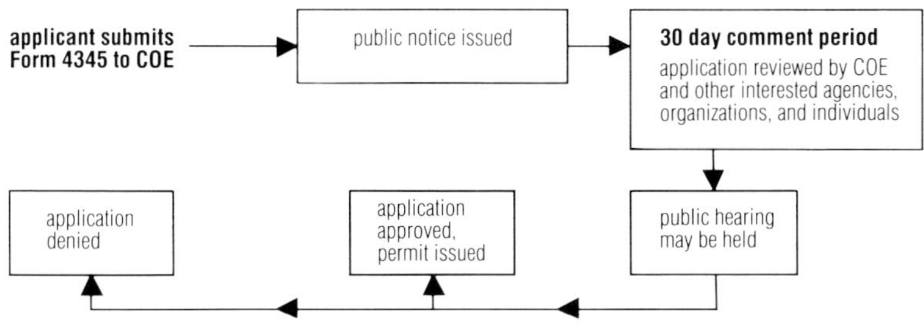

water may be determined by a land survey. Figure 8.1 is a flow chart that illustrates the steps necessary to obtain a permit. Certain projects are exempt from DOE or Office of the Attorney General review, but not necessarily COE review; these include:

- developments worth less than $1000;
- construction of emergency protection structures;
- construction of bulkheads for single family residences;
- construction of noncommercial docks for private use and worth $2500 or less;
- repairs to existing structures.

A well-written permit application for an acceptable project will take a minimum of 68 days to be processed at the local and state levels. Army Corps of Engineers approval requires from 60 to 90 days, but some of this processing time will overlap with the state review period. When an application is denied at the state or local level, grievances among private parties, local officials, and state agencies are settled by a Shoreline Hearings Board, the impartial third party, or ultimately by the State Superior Court. Applications denied by the COE must be negotiated separately with that agency.

Evaluation of Coastal Sites for Development

Determination of the suitability of a coastal site for a development or structural improvement involves technical as well as sociopolitical assessments. The first step in the site evaluation is to make an inventory of the physical and environmental conditions:

- meteorological (precipitation, prevailing wind direction and speed, expected extreme storm wind speed and direction);

- local current regime and wave climate;
- condition and stability of shoreline (rate and prevailing direction of longshore transport, historical changes of shoreline position);
- upland soil characteristics and surficial geology;
- seabed configuration from extreme high water to −10 meters.

Wave Climate

Meteorological data and wave climate assessment go hand-in-hand with bathymetry (depth measurements) since the height, period, and frequency of occurrence of destructive wind waves are determined largely from these three kinds of information. The best method of assessing the wave climate is to obtain long-term measurements at the site over a period when both major storms and average conditions have occurred. Wave height and period estimates can be made, however, using techniques available in the technical literature. The data for this kind of prediction are very simple; one needs only the wind speed and direction curves for the site (COE can supply these for many sites) and a navigation chart (scale larger than 1:150,000).

From these an estimate of the significant wave height and period of wind waves on deep-water fetches can be obtained from graphs in the *Shore Protection Manual.* At locations where the fetch is restricted or sheltered by upland terrain, estimates of significant wave height and period given there may be in error by 7 to 77 percent and −24 to 10 percent, respectively. Such estimates must be used cautiously. For some coastal engineering projects, wave spectra at a site must be predicted. These are necessary for analyses of motion and forces on moored vessels and such structures as buoys, floating breakwaters, and piers. In these situations, the general equation for wind wave spectra can be calibrated with measured field data to yield reasonable spectral estimates. Predicted spectra for the Seacrest Marina site on Elliott Bay, Seattle for various wind speeds are shown in Figure 8.2a.

Vessel wakes also contribute to the wave climate at some coastal sites, particularly sheltered ones with heavy vessel traffic. A study was conducted at Seacrest Marina to examine the wake characteristics of a 94-foot, 1,200-horsepower tugboat. The vessel steamed along courses at various distances from a wave sensor and the wave heights and periods were recorded. At distances of less than 150 meters (500 feet) from the vessel track, the wake was 0.34 to 0.77 meters (1.13 to 2.54 feet) high with an average period of 2.3 seconds. This wake is comparable in height and period to the expected significant wave height and period produced by a 15 meters per second (30 knots) north wind blowing over Elliott Bay. During a typical year, northerly winds with speeds of 15 meters per second blow over Elliott Bay for a total of 44 hours, but persist for only about 6 hours during an individual storm. In a busy

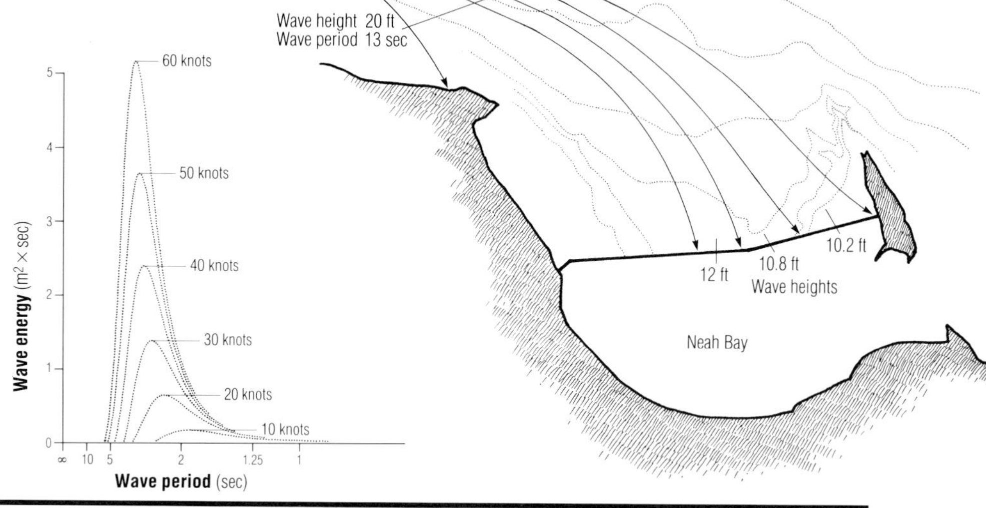

Figure 8.2 Left: Predicted wave energy spectra for various wind speeds at Seacrest Marina, Elliott Bay, King County (from Richey, 1978). Right: Spreading of wave energy and reduction of wave heights at the Neah Bay breakwater caused by refraction.

Puget Sound port, vessel wakes generated on a daily basis must be a design consideration because of the frequency of occurrence and size of the waves involved.

In addition to forecasting the day-to-day wave climate to which a coastal structure will be exposed, a design wave must be determined. The design wave is the engineers' best guess at the largest wave that is likely to influence the structure during its projected life.

In areas of Puget Sound that are sheltered from ocean swell, the design wave can be predicted by extending the wind wave spectral analysis to include winds from the largest storm likely to occur during the project life. For example, the spectra for 25 meters per second (50 knots) winds at the Seacrest Marina, Seattle yield a design deep-water wave 1.3 meters (4.4 feet) high with a period of over 3.2 seconds. At sites exposed to long period waves, the effects of refraction and shoaling must also be included in the design wave analysis. Figure 8.2b shows the site of the Neah Bay breakwater and illustrates the spreading of wave rays and energy at the project location caused by the offshore bathymetry. The design deep-water wave height of 6.1 meters (20 feet) and period of 13 seconds were obtained from offshore wave data. Refracted wave heights are indicated at various sections of the breakwater and it can be seen that the deep-water storm waves diminish in height up to 50 percent because of refraction effects.

Extreme Water Levels

Water level is another fundamental piece of information that is required for evaluating the performance of coastal structures. Normal fluctuations in water level in Puget Sound result from the astronomical tides, seasonal variations in wind direction and the discharge of rivers, and fluctuations in barometric pressure. The annual maximum and minimum astronomical tidal elevations for most sites can be obtained from the U.S. Department of Commerce, NOAA Tide Tables. These elevations vary over an 18-year cycle but only by a few centimeters so that the predictions for any year are representative at most sites. Mean sea level is rising very gradually at the rate of about 20 centimeters (0.66 feet) per century in central Puget Sound and must be considered in the design of a development that is intended to last that long (p. 5).

More immediately important, however, are the short-term extreme high water levels associated with storms since most of the property loss and structural failures caused by wave attack, flooding, and coastal erosion are caused by them.

Five storm-related factors affect water level:

- location of a site relative to the track of the atmospheric pressure disturbance;
- shape of offshore waterways and their orientation with respect to storm wind direction;
- orientation of the shore with respect to the direction of storm wave approach;
- bathymetry of the nearshore zone, primarily the beach slope, and seabed roughness;
- proximity of a site to river mouths.

Most commonly, extreme high water levels occur when the passage of a low-pressure system over the region coincides with high tide. The sea surface rises under the center of the system because of the reduced atmospheric pressure. In addition to the pressure effect, the wind stress on the sea surface accompanying the storm moves water in the direction of the wind and can cause it to accumulate temporarily in enclosed bays. Enclosed waterways such as Port Susan, East Sound–Orcas Island, Case and Carr inlets, and Dabob Bay which open into the direction of storm winds are subject to high water levels from wind stress effects. Water level changes due to the combined effects of surface atmospheric pressure and wind stress are called storm surges and the first two factors above relate to this phenomenon. The astronomical tide, storm surge, and riverine flooding may all combine to raise the still water level at the shore. The third and fourth factors in conjunction with the local wave climate determine the additional and more transient increases in water level produced by wave setup and runup on the beach or on structures that may be located there. These latter effects are the most difficult and time consuming to predict because the factors that control them can vary over longshore distances of 100 meters (328 feet) or less in Puget Sound.

The most reliable method for establishing representative extreme high water levels for a site is to examine long-term tide measurements obtained in the vicinity, which include severe storms. Analyses of this kind have been done for many coastal areas in the region by the COE and the Federal Emergency Management Agency (FEMA) (Table 8.2). Extreme high water level predictions can be obtained from these agencies in the form of maps that show areas subject to coastal flooding.

Floods and Landslides

Statewide property losses in 1974 dollars caused by floods and landslides have been estimated at 25 million and 10 million dollars. Despite these substantial dollar amounts, no state or federal guidelines presently exist to assist the developer or shore property owner in mak-

Table 8.2 Predicted and observed high-water levels for selected coastal locations (relative to mean lower low water).

Location	10-Year (feet)	100-Year (feet)
Clallam County		
Clallam Bay		**12**
Elwha Delta		**12**
Ediz Hook (Base) Outer		**12**
Ediz Hook (End) Outer		**15**
Port Angeles		**11**
Dungeness Delta (Jamestown)		**12**
Jefferson County		
Port Townsend Bay (Hadlock)	**7.5**	**8.2**
Port Ludlow Bay (Port Ludlow)	**8.8**	**10.1**
Port Discovery Bay (Beckett Pt.)	**7.5**	**9.5**
Quilcene Bay (Little Quilcene R.)	**10.1**	**10.8**
Hood Canal (Dosewallips Delta)	**12.2**	**12.6**
Hood Canal (Duckabush Delta)	**11.3**	**11.7**
Island County		
Whidbey Is. (Swantown)	**9.5**	**10.2**
Whidbey Is. (Admiralty Bay)	**11.1**	**11.2**
Possession Sound (Columbia Beach)	9.9	**10.8**
Port Susan (Driftwood Shores)	10.4	**11.4**
Mutiny Bay (Shore Drive)	8.8	**9.3**
Useless Bay	10.6	**11.2**
Lagoon Pt.	8.6	**9.2**
Holmes Harbor (Dines Pt.)	9.0	9.6
Oak Harbor (Marina)	8.2	8.8

Location	10-Year (feet)	100-Year (feet)
Skagit County		
Goat Is.	7.8	**9.8**
Smilk Bay	7.9	8.3
Burrows Bay	6.5	**8.5**
Anacortes	6.7	**8.7**
Cypress Is.	6.6	**7.1**
Padilla Bay	6.9	**8.9**
Samish Bay	6.8	**8.8**
Snohomish County		
Edmonds	8.2	**10.1**
Mukilteo	7.8	**9.8**
Everett	7.9	8.3
Tulalip Bay (Hermosa Pt.)	8.0	**10.0**
Stanwood	7.9	**9.9**
Pierce County		
Browns Pt.	8.6	*8.9*
East Nisqually Delta	9.5	*10.1*
Gig Harbor	9.4	*9.9*
West Side Fox Is.	9.4	*9.9*
Case Inlet (Sunshine Beach)	9.8	*10.1*
Drayton Passage (Amsterdam Bay)	9.5	*10.0*

Bold: Levels include influence of wave setup and runup. Changes in beach profile or structure may alter these levels

Italic: Observed extreme high water levels, December 1977

Source: Data from DOE, FEMA, and COE

Table 8.3 Coastal landforms and the hazards associated with them. Light numbers indicate the relative likelihood of landslides, flooding, etc.; bold numbers indicate the relative level of damage to structures and property.

Hazards due to geological factors[1]

Hazards caused by hydraulic effects

Coastal landforms and features			Soil instability (Liquefaction and differential settling)	Slope instability (Landslides and rockfalls)	Slope instability (Creep)	Flooding (River and stream)	Flooding (Tidal and storm surge)	Erosion (River and stream)	Erosion (Wave and current)
Nearshore	Beaches	Foreshore	1.5/**1.5**						4/**4**
		Backshore	1.5/**2.5**			2/**1**	3/**1**		4/**4**
	Intertidal mudflats		3/**3.5**					3/**2**	4/**2**
Wetlands	Salt marsh, deltas		3/**3.5**			2/**2**	3/**2**	3/**2**	4/**2**
Uplands	Glacial and alluvial sediments	Low bluff[2]	2/**2**	3/**1.5**	1/**1**	2/**1**	3/**2**		4/**3**
		High bluff[3] (beach with backshore)	2/**2**	3/**2.5**	2/**2**				4/**3**
		High bluff (beach, no backshore)	2/**2**	4/**2.5**	3/**2**				4/**4**
	Bedrock	Low cliff[2]		1/**2**	1/**1**	2/**1**	3/**1**		1/**1**
		High cliff[3]		2/**3**	2/**2**				1/**1**

[1] May be initiated by seismic or man-caused ground motion

[2] Less than 3 meters [3] More than 3 meters

Most likely/**Most impact**

ing informed land-use decisions that minimize the risks of losses from coastal hazards. This is not to say that the necessary information does not exist but rather that the responsibility for hazard assessment rests squarely with the property owner or developer.

Table 8.3 is a summary of the hazards discussed in this volume and their associations with easily distinguished coastal landforms and features. It alerts developers to the hazards that might exist at a coastal site and their frequency of occurrence and relative impacts. For example, a site with uplands characterized by high cliffs of bedrock may have hazardous slopes prone to slides and rockfall as well as minor problems due to wave erosion—a comparatively low level of risk. A low-bluff site composed of unconsolidated materials, in contrast, is potentially a more risky area and may have associated with it all types of hazards including flooding, erosion, and slope failure.

Beach and Coastline Stability

Beach and coastline stability is the capability of coastal features to resist changes caused by geological, environmental, or man-made events. If a site is not stable, structural improvements may fail prematurely and may adversely affect the stability of areas adjacent to them as well. Field evidence and historical records, and aerial photograph interpretation are the primary means to assess site stability. Figure 3.1 (p. 34) illustrates costly and unfortunate situations that developed when beach stability was improperly evaluated; they are among many that exist in the region.

Several questions concerning the predevelopment shore conditions can be answered by visiting the site. Figure 8.3 shows a map of a project site at Poverty Bay, south central Puget Sound, and is an example of a field assessment of physical conditions. The proposed development included the installation of a boat launching facility and rehabilitation of an existing pier for public fishing. Information displayed on the site map was collected during a field visit to determine the existing stability of the beach and probable alterations to show conditions that would result from the development. The map shows: (1) distribution of sedimentary materials on the beach (sand, gravel, cobbles, boulders), (2) type and extent of existing erosion control devices, (3) beach profile locations, and (4) indications of erosion and slides.

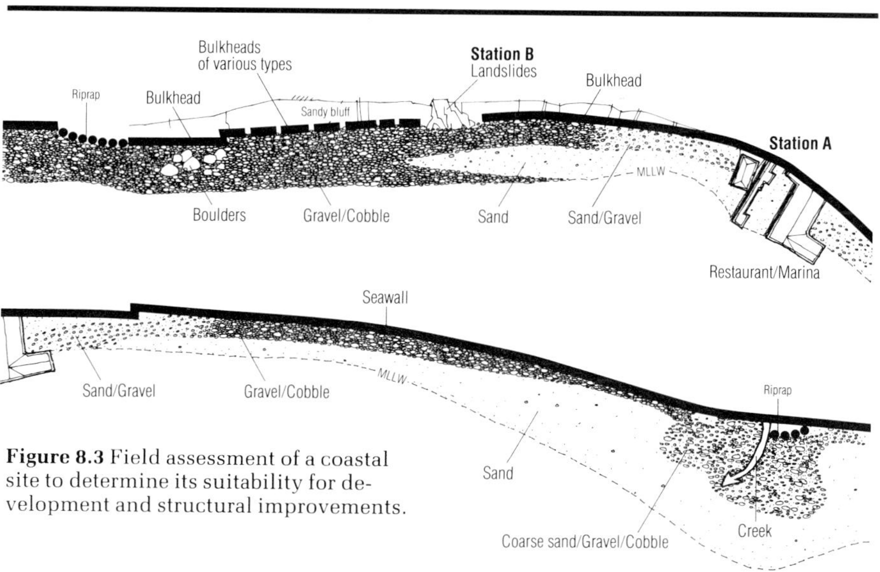

Figure 8.3 Field assessment of a coastal site to determine its suitability for development and structural improvements.

Several conclusions can be drawn from such reconnaissance mapping. The patchy distribution of sand and the underlying gravel-cobble substrate indicate that sand is in transit along this segment of the coast and the site is located on a transport pathway. Since there is very little sand available for transport in the longshore transport cell, extensive sandy beaches have not developed. A small triangular deposit of sand at Station A is evidence that longshore transport is to the south. The landslides located at Station B suggest that the bluffs toward the north of the site were an active source of beach material before the construction of bulkheads along the bluffs. Erosion control devices, bulkheads, and riprap have stabilized the coastline at the expense of the sand supply for the local beach. It was concluded from this and other evidence that a proposed pile-supported pier, being an open structure, would produce little alteration at the project site or along the adjacent shores.

Historical information about past changes of coastline shape can be acquired from old maps and navigational charts, survey party notes, ground photographs, and discussion with long-time residents of the project area. The information supplied by such data provides useful indications of long-term changes for periods of a century or less. The scale of old maps is normally too small to show changes along short segments of beach, however. Old surveys are helpful where survey markers still exist; since estimations of average annual erosion rates can be made from changes in the location of the coastline with respect to these markers. Table 8.4 lists some average annual bluff recession rates determined by this method. The most useful old photographs

Table 8.4 Summary of coastal erosion rates.

Area	Rate (cm/yr)
Strait of Juan de Fuca	60-90[1]
Exposed shores of Whidbey Island	30-165[1]
Penn Cove	10-15[1]
Skagit County	
Rocky shores	0.6[2]
Sand and gravel beaches	5.0[2]
Wave-cut platforms in bedrock	0.1-0.7[2]

[1] Maximum rates. Source: Keuler, personal communication, 1979.

[2] Source: Keuler, 1979.

show the extent and location of beach deposits relative to fixed landmarks: old buildings, piers, pilings or bulkheads, and natural objects such as large rocks or trees. When the season and date of a series of photographs can be documented, seasonal and annual variation of the beach profile can be distinguished.

Personal accounts about historical changes of the coastline generally provide the least quantitative evidence because they rarely include physical measurements and there is uncertainty about the exact dates of relevant events or how dramatic the changes really were. Nonetheless, they are valuable in conjunction with other information. Some topics about which shore residents should be questioned include:

- chronic erosion difficulties and corrective remedies used;
- location and dates of fill or excavation projects and the approximate volumes of material involved;
- major storms and flood levels or structural damage caused by them.

As an example of the value of personal accounts, consider the two aerial photographs of Mutiny Bay, Whidbey Island taken in 1957 and 1972 (Fig. 8.4). Analysis of these photographs alone would indicate that the inlet and tidal embayment in the 1972 photograph were closed

Figure 8.4 Vertical air photos of the coastal zone at Mutiny Bay, Whidbey Island. The tidal inlet in the 1957 photo was filled for a development.

by longshore growth of the spit at its mouth. This misinterpretation was avoided when local residents pointed out that the area had been filled for development.

An extensive set of vertical aerial photographs dating back to 1936 is available for many areas of the Puget Sound region. During the last decade, the COE has flown annual (except 1971 and 1975) coastal environment surveillance flights and copies of their photographs can be obtained at reasonable cost. Other governmental agencies, Washington State Departments of Ecology and Natural Resources, as well as private companies, maintain libraries of aerial photographs that can be obtained either on loan or for a fee.

Figure 8.5 illustrates the results of an air photo study for a small project in central Puget Sound. The question to be resolved was whether or not constructions at the beach had caused any change in the trend of coastal erosion and deposition on the spit at Miller Creek. The analysis showed that cyclic events of growth and retreat of the spit had been occurring long before the shore was developed. It was concluded that present-day erosion of the spit is a natural fluctuation of the coastline that is unrelated to activities at the site.

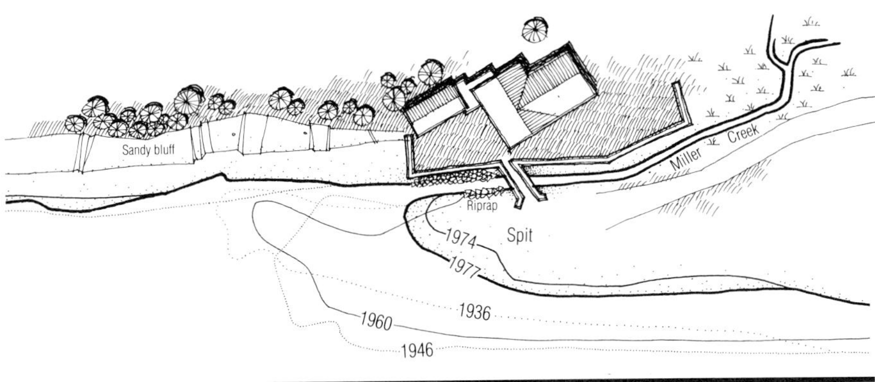

Figure 8.5 Cycles of erosion and growth of a small spit revealed by air photo analysis.

Another example of air photo interpretation is shown in Figure 8.6. In this example a large rock revetment was constructed to protect a sludge storage pond from wave attack. Since the structure extended about 100 meters (328 feet) across the preexisting beach and blocked longshore transport, the question was whether or not it affected beach stability and sedimentation at the site. Historical evidence indicated that the south shore of West Point, Seattle had been quite stable for more than 80 years before the revetment was installed in 1962–1963.

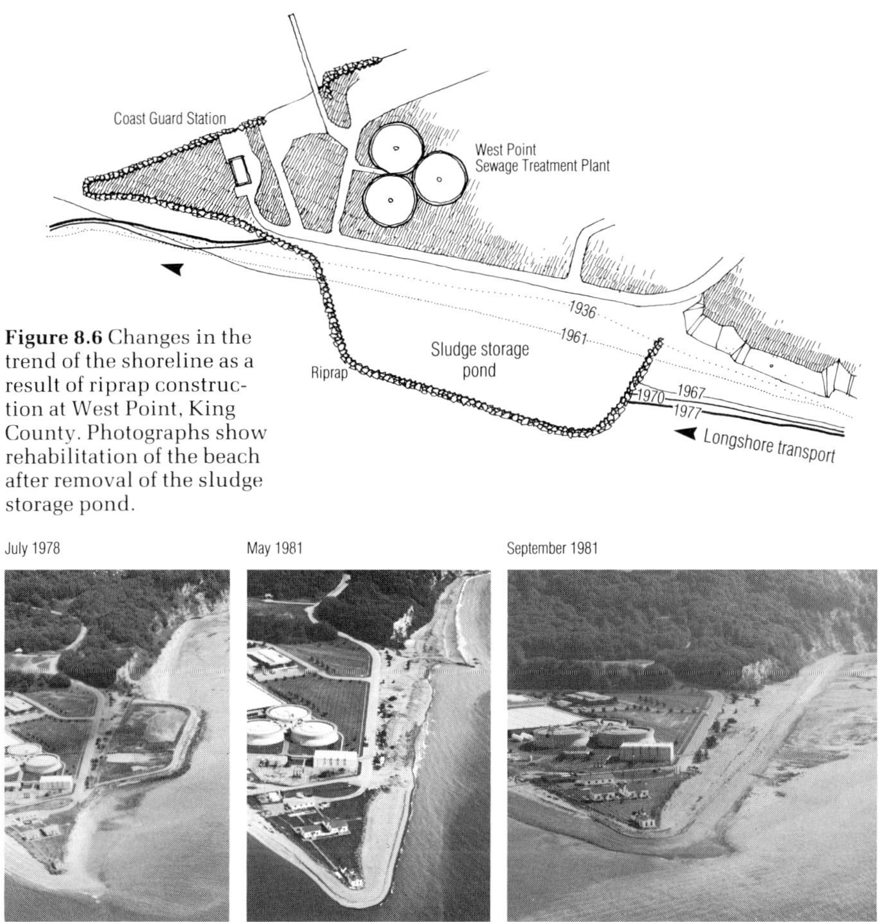

Figure 8.6 Changes in the trend of the shoreline as a result of riprap construction at West Point, King County. Photographs show rehabilitation of the beach after removal of the sludge storage pond.

Since that time a sandy pocket beach accreted at the southeast end of the revetment and the predominant direction of longshore transport, therefore, is from south to north at this site. Based on the volume of material deposited between 1963 and 1967 when sand began to pass by the structure, an average annual longshore transport rate of 765 cubic meters (1,000 cubic yards) per year was estimated. Concurrent with the pocket beach accretion at the updrift (southeast) end of the revetment, there was a loss of beach material from the northwest (downdrift) end of the structure produced by the reduced supply of sand. Erosion, however, decreased about four years after the project was completed because sand then bypassed the revetment and there was adequate riprap to protect the low-lying backshore. The revetment was removed in 1981 and the shore rehabilitated with an artificial gravel beach retained by a short gravel and rock groin at the downdrift end. The performance of the artificial beach in the next decade will help provide valuable and long-needed information about beach restoration in Puget Sound.

Controlling Coastal Erosion

Coastal erosion is a natural process by which the beaches lose material that moves offshore or supplies other beaches in the local area. Typically, erosion is manifested by a chronic and gradual loss of upland area. Since bluff recession rates can be up to 1.5 meters (5 feet) per year and developed shorefront property can be valued at one to two thousand dollars per lineal foot, residential property owners understandably view the process as a serious and costly threat to the value of their real estate. In some instances the onset of an erosion problem can be both sudden and severe and emergency measures are required to reduce financial losses. For example, storms in 1967 and 1970 produced damage to the Crown Zellerbach facilities on Ediz Hook totaling $30,000 and $100,000 respectively. There are numerous solutions to erosion problems, and these vary in complexity from planting vegetation to building massive concrete structures. The crux of the problem is to reduce the loss of shore property to an acceptable degree without disturbing the supply of sediment to adjacent beaches. Some remedies used in Puget Sound are described in the following pages and a comparison of their features and relative costs is given in Table 8.6.

Nonstructural Remedies

The most economical and environmentally sound way to cope with an erosion problem is to avoid it. New structures should be set far enough back from the edge of a receding bluff so that they are not affected by erosion during their projected life. Unfortunately, this is not done by many coastal residents because their view of the Sound and the value of their property would be impaired. Construction setback, however, does have advantages: the natural process of bluff erosion and beach nourishment continues; beach flora and fauna are not disturbed and remain to be enjoyed in their natural state.

Vegetation

Vegetation is another nonstructural line of defense against erosion. Plants are quite effective at stabilizing the backshore, upland slopes, and dunes in locations where erosion is not very severe. Plant foliage shelters soil surfaces from the impact of rain and sea-spray. Tree and shrub roots bind loose materials together into the soil profile and reduce their tendency to creep downslope. Vegetation is a self-maintained, low-cost, and renewable form of erosion control whose application does not require a permit under the Shoreline Management Act.

There has been considerable experimentation with the use of vegetation for erosion control in other parts of the country but little is known of its effectiveness in Puget Sound. The Corps of Engineers has published guidelines for the selection of appropriate plant species,

Figure 8.7 Beach grass planted to stabilize an artificial beach at West Point, King County.

transplanting procedures, optimal planting times, and estimated costs of various treatments. Some of this information is applicable to local problems.

Beach grass was planted on the backshore of the artificial beach at West Point (Fig. 8.7). As part of a larger experiment to evaluate low-cost erosion control structures at Oak Harbor, Whidbey Island, the COE planted a variety of native ground cover, Hookers willow, as well as introduced species of snow berry, ocean spray, wild rose, and European beachgrass on fill material behind its experimental structures. The purpose of the planting was to determine the colonization rates and ground holding capabilities of these species. The experiment was ended prematurely by the February 1979 storm which heavily damaged the erosion control test structures retaining the fill. Tall wheat grass, planted on the fill that remained after the storm, appears to be doing very well. Future experiments of this type will provide useful information on erosion control with vegetation adapted to this region.

The U.S. Department of Agriculture Soil Conservation Technical Services Division maintains the Plant Material Center at Corvallis, Oregon. Various aspects of aquatic plant propagation are evaluated at the center and a limited inventory of plant materials is available for experimental use. Individuals and community groups considering vegetation as a means of erosion control are encouraged to contact the USDA center for technical advice.

Beach Nourishment

Augmenting the natural supply of beach sediment is an effective means of controlling shore recession. Beach nourishment has been used effectively for many decades in other parts of the United States but has been applied to Puget Sound beaches only recently. Nourishment projects are currently in progress at Ediz Hook, Sunnyside Beach near Steilacoom, and at West Point in Seattle.

Beach nourishment is more attractive than structural methods because the aesthetic value of the beach is preserved and the supply of sand to beaches downdrift is improved. Nourishment is not always practical, however, because fill material can be very expensive to apply. Moreover, the buried beach flora and fauna may never completely reestablish themselves. Beach nourishment, like structural erosion control projects, requires a permit.

Several factors must be investigated in determining the feasibility of beach nourishment. A sediment budget for the site must be established so that the yearly rate of beach erosion can be determined (Fig. 4.7, p. 48). Long-term survey data provide the most accurate basis for determining these rates, but such data are usually unavailable or are costly to obtain. The volume of fill material required must be estimated from shoreline recession rates and beach changes observable in other historical data. A useful rule of thumb for estimating the material supply rate and the economics of a nourishment project is that one cubic yard of fill material similar in size to the beach sediment should be added per square foot of beach area to be rehabilitated.

Since the size characteristics of fill material (proportions of sand and gravel) usually do not match the natural beach sediment exactly, additional fill is required to compensate for the silt, clay, and sand that the waves wash from the fill immediately after it is placed on the beach. Table 8.5 lists the volumes of various fill materials necessary to restore a unit volume of beach at Ediz Hook. Applying the above rule of thumb, one foot of eroded beach along a 30-meter (100-foot) section will require 95 cubic meters (125 cubic yards) of upland pit-run gravel per year for initial restoration.

Nourishment is not a permanent solution to erosion problems and material must be reapplied periodically to maintain a stable beach. Project costs for the initial rehabilitation and maintenance include procurement and hauling of fill and its placement on the beach, and replenishment requirements. Because of its erosion resistance, coarse fill material is most economical. Possible losses of shellfish beds, spawning areas, primary production, and recreational value of a beach must be carefully assessed before replenishment with coarse material is considered. Coarse material also steepens beach slopes significantly.

Ediz Hook Case (page 49) Beach nourishment at Ediz Hook has two purposes. First, the added material will protect the revetment erosion control structure from being undercut by waves and second, the natural character of the beach will be preserved. For economic reasons, coarse material was selected for the Ediz Hook beach nourishment project. Cobbles and coarse gravel from an upland barrow site were placed on the lower beach face. Stockpiles of feed material were graded after placement, but only to a limited degree, since it was anticipated that

Figure 8.8 Fate of beach feed material placed on Ediz Hook, Clallam County, and beach profile changes (from Corps of Engineers).

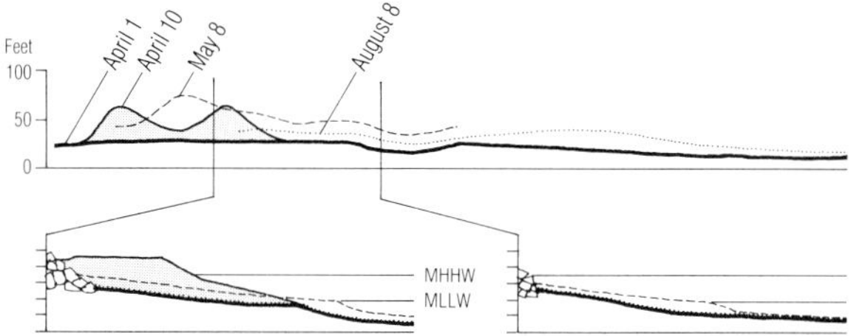

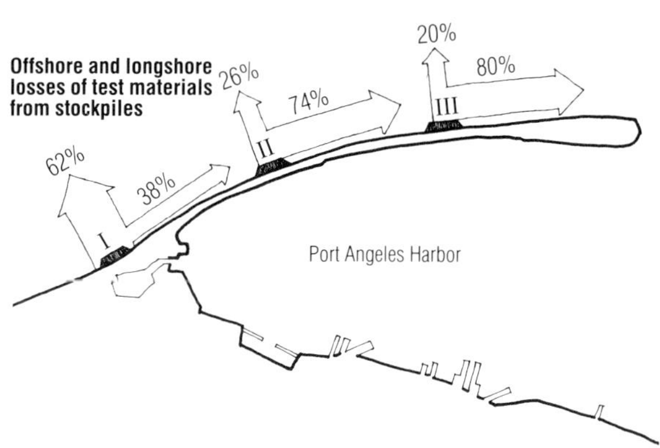

Table 8.5 Ediz Hook overfill ratios by type and source of beach feed material (cubic yards per cubic yard of beach)

Offshore sediments	
Taken near base of Ediz Hook	2.4
Taken near end of Ediz Hook	2.25
Upland gravel	
Pit run gravel	1.25
Processed gravel (diameter, one inch and larger)	0.9

wave action would complete the even dispersal of material along the beach.

Preconstruction tests with the nourishment material indicated that the waves dispersed the feed material rapidly. Figure 8.8 shows the dispersion of feed material from stockpiles after its placement. Initial erosion rates were about 500 cubic meters (650 cubic yards)/month per 30 meters (100 feet) of beach but after 3 months the rates decreased 62 percent to about 191 cubic meters (250 cubic yards)/month per 30 meters. Reduced erosion resulted when the stockpiles of fill developed a natural and stable beach profile. Most of the initial loss of fill material was offshore at site I (62 percent), but only 26 percent and 20 percent moved offshore from sites II and III (Fig. 8.8b). The balance of offshore versus longshore losses of beach material at various locations on Ediz Hook reflects the longshore variation in wave energy produced by refraction (Fig. 4.8) and the orientation of the beach with respect to the direction of wave approach (pp. 48–49). About 15,000 cubic meters (20,000 cubic yards) of fill will be required annually to maintain the beach and protect the revetment. Renourishment is provided in 5-year installments and the fill requirements will be adjusted in response to the beach conditions that develop during each installment.

Sunnyside Beach Case In the early 1900s a low, 5-acre headland was constructed immediately north of Steilacoom, Pierce County with waste sand from a nearby gravel pit. A beach 305 meters (1,000 feet) long by 30 meters (100 feet) wide formed along the shore of the headland. The town of Steilacoom constructed a park on the headland in the 1920s and more recently a sewage treatment plant as well. The headland is now in jeopardy because the beach which once protected it from erosion began to recede in the 1940s and 1950s and bank erosion rates near the sewage treatment plant are about 0.9 meters (3 feet) per year. An estimated 900 cubic yards of material are lost from the beach and headland annually. A 170-meter (550-foot) timber bulkhead installed in 1967 failed to stop bank recession and a beach nourishment program was begun to save the headland.

In 1975 the town of Steilacoom placed 13,800 cubic meters (18,000 cubic yards) of sand on the lower beach face from a barge and landscaped the beach profile with bulldozers at low tide. Despite these measures, COE surveys indicated that Sunnyside Beach was still eroding at a moderate rate. Consequently, an additional 3,200 cubic meters (4,200 cubic yards) of sand were placed on the beach in 1978. The fate of the most recent fill is being monitored, but the unsatisfactory performance of initial nourishment suggests that the fill material may not have been suitably resistant to the wave climate and nearshore currents on the beach. Had coarser fill material been selected initially, the beach nourishment might have been more successful.

Bypassing

Structures such as breakwaters, jetties, and groins can interrupt or permanently stop the natural longshore movement of sediment. These barriers cause beach accretion on the updrift side and beach erosion on the downdrift side, altering the sediment supply. This situation developed at West Point as discussed earlier (p. 99). At an exposed site, the erosion of the downdrift segment can damage the structure foundation and result in loss of upland areas. An effective and cost efficient method of rehabilitation is to transfer material accreted on the updrift side to the eroding beach.

The dredged channel and attached breakwater constructed at Keystone Harbor on Whidbey Island in 1948 interrupted sediment movement along the beach on the north shore of Admiralty Bay. This site is exposed to a long fetch to the south and waves move approximately 4,975 cubic meters (6,500 cubic yards) of material per year to it from Admiralty Head. Dredging on a 4- to 5-year cycle is required to remove this material from the channel. The beach to the east of the breakwater is deprived of material and has eroded at rates ranging from 4.6 to 12.2 meters (15 to 40 feet) per year, causing damage to the landward end of the breakwater on several occasions (Fig. 8.9). Since 1960, the dredged material has been placed on the east beach to provide an artificial sediment source for the beaches downdrift from the harbor. The bypassing operation has established a balance between the rates of dredging and erosion on the east beach and appears to be effectively controlling the critical erosion at the base of the breakwater. The east beach still retreats about 6.1 meters (20 feet) per year between dredging operations, but fluctuations of this nature are characteristic of beaches undergoing periodic nourishment.

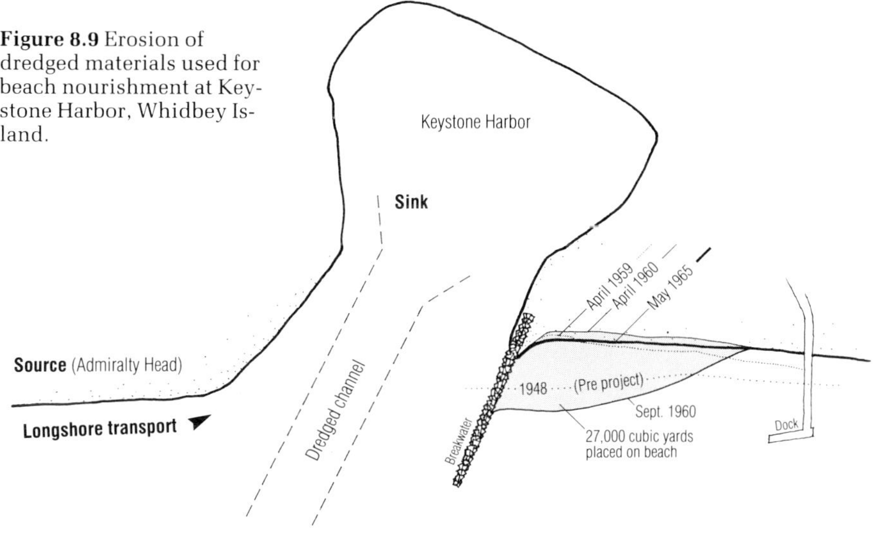

Figure 8.9 Erosion of dredged materials used for beach nourishment at Keystone Harbor, Whidbey Island.

Drift Logs

Maverick sawlogs, escapees from storage and towing booms, lumber, and whole trees uprooted and delivered to Puget Sound by flooding rivers are abundant and widely dispersed on beaches throughout the region. These materials become stranded on the backshore during high spring and storm tides. Drift logs form semipermanent stockpiles which trap beach sediment and promote the establishment of vegetation on beaches with large berms (Fig. 8.10). Once partially covered with sediment, logs form a partial wave barrier. Natural protection of shore bluffs is provided by drift logs in this manner along many undeveloped beaches in Puget Sound. On other beaches, logs create natural traps for sand moved by wind and waves. Deposits of wind-blown sand 0.5 to 1.0 meters (1.6–3.3 feet) above the extreme high water level can form in this way.

Beaches without berms, on the contrary, often are affected adversely by drift logs. These beaches typically are armored with algae-covered gravel and cobble. This surface is both durable and slippery so that logs skid over it rather than scour into it as they do in a sandy beach face. In this situation, the logs can become battering rams when moved by storm waves at high tide. Without a cushion of sand to slow them, logs can excavate large quantities of sediment from the bluff and make it available for transport along the beach. For example, a 10-meter (32-foot) sawlog 0.5 meter (20 inches) in diameter that has been in the water for a while weighs about 2,050 kilograms (4,500 pounds). When this log is moving at 2 feet per second in a breaking wave, it can deliver 9,000-foot pounds of energy when it collides with a rigid structure end-on (Fig. 8.10). Although most drift logs wash ashore peacefully during calm sea conditions, their more violent nature during storms must be considered along with other extreme forces when designing coastal structures.

Structural Remedies

A variety of structural devices is employed to stabilize erosion-prone beaches and shore bluffs. The devices range in sophistication from ingenious homemade structures of drift logs to massive seawalls constructed of steel-reinforced concrete (Fig. 8.10). They fall into three general categories according to how they protect the shoreline. The most common device is the bulkhead or seawall. This is a vertical, shore-parallel structure that serves two purposes. First, a bulkhead retains the preexisting bank material as well as any backfill placed behind it; and second, the bulkhead is a rigid barrier that protects filled areas or existing ground from the direct impacts of breaking waves.

A second category of structures includes revetments. These consist of individually emplaced pieces of stone, precast concrete, or other massive materials which are assembled on the beach to form a sloping mat parallel with the shore. Unlike bulkheads, revetments absorb wave energy by providing a porous, rough surface to dissipate wave runup as well as to drain water off the beach. The third type of structure is the groin; and in contrast to the previous two devices, groins are constructed perpendicular to the shoreline. They are low walls, usually less than 0.5 meter (20 inches) above the beach profile, that trap sediment as it moves along the beach. Typically groins are installed in groups, called groin fields, along an eroding stretch of beach. Figure 8.10 shows a groin field that was installed at Birch Bay in the 1930s.

Most bulkheads are installed by private property owners, but prior to the Shoreline Management Act (SMA) of 1971 very little information concerning bulkhead siting and design practice appropriate to Puget Sound was available. Since then, the situation has greatly improved. In 1978 the COE began to evaluate erosion control devices of low to moderate cost and the Washington State Department of Ecology (DOE) sponsored a regional study of erosion control. Both of these programs were designed to provide useful background information for private individuals experiencing critical erosion problems. These agencies as well as the Washington State Department of Fisheries and local county planning organizations should be consulted for advice when an erosion control device appears to be required.

Shoreline protection measures are most successful when owners of adjacent property coordinate efforts to control erosion because the results are more effective in terms of cost per lineal foot, durability of the structure, and continuity of its appearance. Although the general guidelines provided by local, state, and federal agencies can help to solve many planning and design problems associated with erosion control, they are not a substitute for professional engineering services. An engineer experienced in coastal engineering principles can help reduce the risk of structural failure by designing protection for the conditions specific to the site. Historically, many devices installed by private landowners and developers were designed by upland contractors with little knowledge of coastal processes and associated hazards at the water's edge.

Figure 8.10 Examples of structures used for erosion control. Upper left: Stumps and drift wood placed at the edge of an eroding patio. Upper right: Concrete groins on Birch Bay, Whatcom County. Lower left: Wooden post bulkhead, Juniper Beach, Island County. Lower right: Steel reinforced concrete piling, west of Ediz Hook, Clallam County.

Bulkheads and Seawalls

These structures are the least in harmony with the natural processes that occur on the beach and generally are the most costly of the structural alternatives for controlling erosion. Nevertheless, bulkheads are the most frequently selected device installed on our local shores because they are considered by many engineers and property owners to be the ultimate brute-force solution to erosion problems.

There are situations, however, where the fill retention and durability requirements make a bulkhead the only feasible solution. Bulkheads have two attractive features. First, they take up minimal space on the beach and adjacent upland because they are vertical structures. Second, a properly designed bulkhead on an appropriate site is a relatively permanent solution that requires little maintenance. To limit the loss of fish and shellfish resources, the Washington State Department of Fisheries (WDF) has established elevations below which bulkheads and toe protection may not be constructed. These are set forth in WDF (1971) and should be reviewed before the design of a bulkhead or seawall is begun.

A variety of materials can be used in the construction of a bulkhead. Some of the options are shown in Figure 8.11. Many people think reinforced concrete is the most durable; however, examples of its inherent weaknesses are prevalent around Puget Sound. The seawall at Swantown, Whidbey Island (p. 34) was a formidable but improperly designed structure that cost more than $200 per lineal foot to construct. It was undermined by storm waves and collapsed a few months after construction; and the filled area behind the seawall was eroded by waves rendering the site useless for the planned development. The failure of this structure illustrates the major weakness of concrete, its low tensile strength. Because of this property, concrete structures that span long sections of beach will fail unless adequately reinforced with steel and provided with a wide footing on soil with stable and uniform load-bearing characteristics.

Another common mode of bulkhead failure is seaward buckling caused by the increased earth pressure produced when the groundwater level rises behind the structure. Hydrostatic pressure and the weight of fill material can topple impermeable concrete walls onto the beach when drainage of groundwater through them is not provided.

The depth of the footing is also critical for survival of a concrete structure. Wave energy at high tide is dissipated explosively at the structure face and much of it is reflected back onto the beach face in front of the wall, causing scour depressions up to 0.6 meter (2 feet) deep at the toe of the bulkhead. This must be anticipated, and a deep toe trench provided for the footing to accommodate postconstruction erosion of the beach profile. Rock revetment or riprap is often added at the toe to protect the footing from scour but, to be effective, this material must be placed on a size-graded bed of cobbles and gravel to prevent it from shifting down the beach. Figure 8.11 shows sketches of two concrete bulkheads constructed by private property owners. These bulkheads are structurally sound except that the location of the steel reinforcement is not optimally located to prevent tensional failure at the junction of the wall and footing. Also, neither of the footings is placed far enough below the existing beach level to accommodate beach scour. As a general rule, a concrete structure has no more integrity than the footing that supports it.

Wood is an excellent construction material for bulkheads because it is compliant and responds elastically when impacted. It is easily transported and can be assembled on the beach without heavy equipment. Also, a wood bulkhead is more easily repaired because damaged sections can be replaced. Pressure treatment of the wood with preservative compounds will greatly prolong the life of the structure.

Unlike concrete bulkheads which are gravity structures that rely primarily on their own mass and earth pressure on the footing to prevent slippage and overturning, wooden bulkheads are supported by vertical posts deeply buried in the beach. Additional lateral support is provided by tying the upper ends of the posts to "deadman" anchors in the backfill. Design sketches of the log post and used tire bulkheads constructed at Oak Harbor by the COE are shown in Figure 8.11. Wall timbers also may be set vertically and supported by longitudinal wales. This scheme requires that a more extensive trench be excavated to accommodate the vertical timbers, and it should include tiebacks anchored in the backfill to restrain the bulkhead against outward earth pressures.

Wooden structures with tightly fitted timbers may also require drainage if groundwater seepage behind them is excessive. A major result of the COE study was that a filter of plastic cloth or gravel is essential to prevent loss of backfill material through permeable devices. The importance of this design requirement is illustrated on page 65. The damage to the COE test devices evident in these photographs was caused by the erosion of backfill by wave overwash draining through open timber and panel joints during the February 1979 storm. Without the support of backfill, the timber facings were easily smashed by breaking waves and drift logs.

Adjacent and similarly constructed devices performed better because gravel and plastic cloth filters prevented the loss of fill material. Of these two filters, the plastic cloth proved superior at retaining backfill material. Gravel filters reduced the loss of fill significantly but were not completely satisfactory. Another result of the COE study was that 6- to 10-inch diameter angular rock (shot rock) proved inadequate for protection of the toe of the structures during the storm. It shifted down the beach face leaving the structure base exposed to wave attack.

Revetments and Riprap

Revetment wall surfaces are designed to be rough or stair-stepped and porous so that waves will break on them slowly. Most of the wave energy is dissipated harmlessly in driving the water up the rough slope through which it drains back down to the beach. Very little of the energy is reflected offshore to scour the beach. Because of its availability, the most common construction material is large angular rocks called riprap. Extensive riprap protects the railroads along the eastern shore of central Puget Sound between Seattle and Everett.

Design sketches of low-cost revetments evaluated by the COE at Oak Harbor are shown in Figure 8.11. One example is terraced courses of cement-filled bags which were stacked on a 1:1 slope and cured in place. Toe protection consisting of shot rock and a cloth filter were provided. Since the cement revetment is nearly impermeable, 2-inch diameter plastic drain pipes were placed through the base of the device on 10-inch centers.

Gabion mats were also tested at Oak Harbor (Fig. 8.11). These are heavy wire, rock-filled bags, rectangular in shape, that are laid in mats on the beach face. They are usually laid on a gravel bed and provided with a gravel or cloth filter. After the wire bags are assembled, they are filled with cobbles and covered with wire mesh. The base of the gabions is set in a trench to prevent shifting and protected at the toe with shot rock. A feature of both cement bag and gabion mat revetments attractive to the private property owner is the ease with which they can be assembled. Once the materials have been hauled to the beach, walls can be emplaced without heavy equipment. Gabions are compliant and can flex and shift about without rupturing when pounded by waves; they also can be repaired in sections when damaged. The major objections to revetments are that considerable beach area must be used for their construction; and they are less appealing aesthetically than other alternatives.

The cement bag revetments (Fig. 8.11) proved the most durable structure in the February 1979 storm. Waves overtopped them for several hours and pounded them with large drift logs and other debris and yet the face of the structure stood up well to the pounding. Large quantities of fill material were eroded from behind the gabion mats, since the plastic cloth was not an effective filter when used with these permeable structures. Coarser backfill and better filters may be required to improve their durability. Similar problems are experienced with riprap and many of the rocks end up well down the beach face where they provide little erosion protection.

Figure 8.11 Erosion control structures

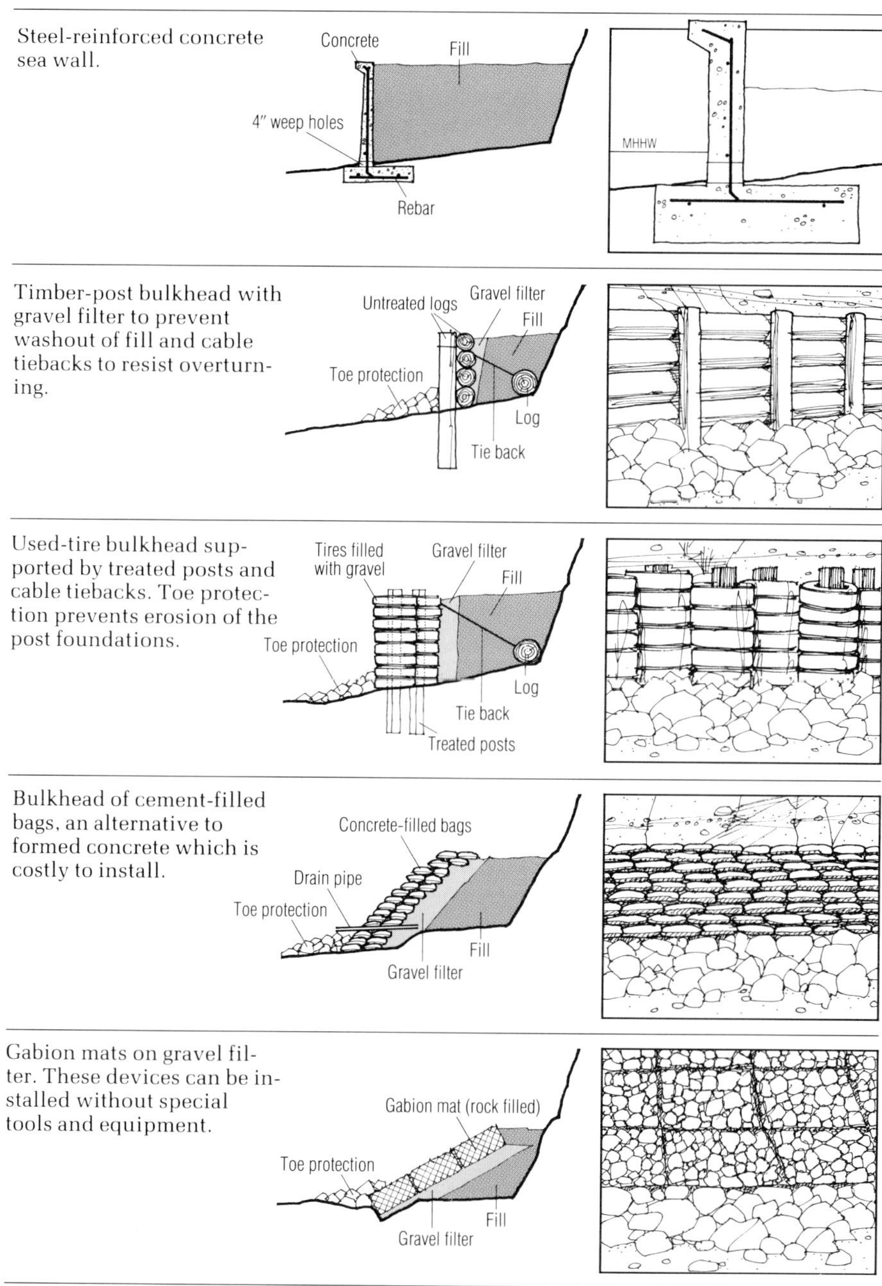

Method of erosion control	Advantage to property owner					Disadvantage to property owner					Advantage to beach/ecosystem			Disadvantage to beach/ecosystem		
	Stops upland erosion	Improves scenic value of beach	Low maintenance cost	Reduces risk of landslide, improves slope stability	Beach accretes rapidly	Does not stop erosion	Reduces scenic value or view	Requires maintenance	Subject to failure	May result in legal problems	Does not impede supply of beach material	Does not destroy benthic habitat	Improves natural supply of sand	Reduces supply of sand	Destroys benthic habitat	Promotes beach erosion seaward of structure
Construction setback		●	●	●		●					●	●				
Vegetation				●		●		●			●	●				
Beach nourishment	●	●		●	●			●			●		●		●	
Bulkhead/ Seawall	●		●	●			●		●	●				●	●	●
Revetment/ Gabion	●		●	●			●		●	●				●	●	
Groin			●		●	●	●		●	●				●	●	

Initial cost (1981 dollars)

Construction setback: Varies with cost of land required to accommodate setback

Vegetation: Minor

Beach nourishment: Cost of material needed to fill beach to 15 feet with an overfill ratio of 1.5 is $90 per linear foot of beach

Bulkhead/Seawall: Wood construction is $104 per linear foot of beach; concrete construction is $100-$680 per linear foot of beach

Revetment/Gabion: Cement bags are $133 per linear foot of beach; wire bags are $97 per linear foot of beach

Groin: Wood construction is $14-$34 per linear foot of structure; concrete construction is $40-$110 per linear foot of structure

Table 8.6 Summary of the advantages and disadvantages of various shore protection alternatives and their initial costs in 1981 dollars.

Groins

To provide effective erosion control, a groin field must have an adequate supply of beach sand. Ideally, sand transported along the shore fills the updrift side of each groin until it can pass by to fill the next groin downdrift. Once the groin field is filled with sand to capacity, longshore transport will continue downdrift to neighboring beaches. An appropriately placed groin field is rapidly buried by the beach accretion it promotes and effectively increases the length and area of the upper beach face. In this way, it has the desired effect of protecting the backshore from direct wave attack.

Grain fields are generally ineffective in Puget Sound because there is not enough longshore transport to make them function properly (Fig. 8.10). Inappropriately sited groins aggravate the erosion problems experienced by the owners of adjacent property by reducing critically low longshore transport. Many lawsuits have been fought over this type of problem. In addition, groins eventually deteriorate into unsightly deposits of rubble where inadequately supplied with sediment. For most Puget Sound beaches, groins are not considered to be an effective erosion control device.

Conclusion

The preceding chapters have traced the evolution of the coast of Puget Sound from its early postglacial history to its present-day development. Being the first summary yet prepared, this book is an introduction to problems that will have to be solved as development accelerates: it is best used as a basis for future investigations. As programs to assess environmental aspects of the coast that were initiated in the 1970s are concluded and the information from them put to use and field tested, the extent of knowledge will be enhanced greatly. With understanding of the natural processes that have created the coastline and knowledge of the kinds of development that are beneficial to it, citizens and developers will be better prepared to enjoy the coast as it is, or to alter it in a responsible manner. It will be challenging for all concerned to watch these changes occur and to participate in the management of these precious resources.

Glossary

Abrasion Grinding of rock by wave-agitated sand and gravel.

Accretion The growth of a beach by the addition of material transported by wind and water.

Alluvium Clay, silt, sand, and gravel deposited by streams and rivers.

Backshore Upper part of the beach between the beach face and the coastline; affected by severe storm waves.

Backwash The seaward return of water following the uprush of a breaking wave.

Bar A shallow-water deposit of sand, gravel, or other unconsolidated material formed on the sea floor by waves and currents.

Bay mouth bar A bar extending partly or entirely across the mouth of a bay.

Beach The zone of unconsolidated material that is moved by waves, wind, and tidal currents, extending landward to the coastline.

Beach erosion The removal of beach materials by waves, tidal and nearshore currents, or wind.

Beach face The section of the beach normally exposed to the action of wave uprush.

Beach nourishment The process of replenishing a beach with sedimentary material.

Beach profile A vertical cross section of a beach perpendicular to the shoreline.

Beach scarp A steep slope produced by wave erosion.

Bedload A highly concentrated layer of sediment rolled along the seabed by waves and currents.

Berm The nearly horizontal portion of the backshore formed by backwash, usually above mean higher high water (MHHW).

Breakwater A structure protecting a shore area, harbor, or anchorage from waves.

Bulkhead A retaining wall along the shore to protect the uplands from waves.

Bypassing The transfer of beach material from the updrift side of an inlet or harbor entrance to the downdrift side.

Capillary wave Water wave caused by surface tension and less than three centimeters long.

Coastal zone The land and sea area bordering the shoreline.

Coastline The line where terrestrial processes give way to marine processes, tidal currents, wind waves, etc.

Cusp Rounded low deposits of beach material separated by crescent-shaped troughs.

Datum A horizontal reference plane for water level measurements. A tidal datum is defined by a specific phase of the tide.

Debris line A line marking the landward limit of debris moved by storm waves.

Deep water Water so deep that surface waves are little affected by the ocean bottom, generally one-half the surface wave length.

Delta A deposit of sediment formed at a river mouth.

Detritus Sedimentary material derived from the weathering of solid rock.

Dolphin A cluster of piles bound together.

Downdrift The direction of movement of beach materials.

Dunes Ridges or mounds of wind-blown sand.

Duration The length of time the wind blows in the same direction without obstruction.

Eddy A circular movement of water formed on the side of a main current. Eddies may be created at points where the main stream passes obstructions or between two adjacent currents flowing in opposite directions.

Erosion The wearing away of land by the action of natural forces.

Estuary The region near a river mouth where fresh water and salt water mix.

Extreme high water The high water level that can be expected to occur once in a 50- to 100-year period.

Fetch length The horizontal distance along open water over which the wind blows and generates waves.

Foreshore The beach between mean higher high and mean lower low water levels.

Groin A structure built perpendicular to the shoreline to protect against erosion and to trap sand.

Headland A high steep-faced point of land extending into the sea.

Hook A spit or narrow cape of sand or gravel which turns landward at its outer end.

Igneous rock Rock formed of once molten minerals.

Jetty A structure extending into the water to protect a harbor or to direct tidal currents.

Kinetic energy Energy associated with motion.

Lagoon A shallow water body connected to the sea.

Levee A dike or embankment which protects land from floods.

Littoral Living on, or occurring on, the shore.

Littoral drift The mud, sand, or gravel material moved in the nearshore zone by waves and currents.

Longshore Parallel with the shoreline.

Longshore bar A sandbar parallel with the shoreline which is submerged at high tide.

Longshore current The wave-generated current in the nearshore zone flowing parallel with the shore.

Longshore transport rate The rate at which sedimentary material is moved along the shore by waves and currents; usually expressed in cubic yards (or meters) per year.

Low-tide terrace A broad flat portion of the beach profile located near the mean lower low water level.

Mean higher high water (MHHW) The average height of the higher high waters over a 19-year period.

Mean lower low water (MLLW) The average height of the lower low waters over a 19-year period.

Mean sea level The average height of the surface of the sea over a 19-year period, usually determined from hourly tide gauge measurements.

Metamorphic rock Rock formed from sediment or igneous material that has been subjected to high pressure or temperature.

Nearshore circulation The water circulation along the shore produced by waves, wind, and tidal forces.

Nearshore current A current in the nearshore zone generated by the combined effects of waves, wind, and tides.

Nearshore zone An indefinite zone extending seaward from the shoreline well beyond the breaker zone, defining the area in which water and sedimentary material are moved by wave action.

Outfall A large pipe for discharging sewage or waste water into lakes, rivers, or the ocean.

Percolation Water seepage through spaces between sediment particles or through porous structures.

Potential energy Energy associated with position, usually elevation.

Propagation of waves The passage of waves through water.

Quarrying Extraction of bedrock or sedimentary material by air or water pressures in breaking waves.

Quaternary The last two million years, the most recent geologic period of the Cenozoic Era.

Refraction diagram A chart of wave crest or ray positions for a specific deep-water wave period and direction.

Residual deposit Coarse sediment, most commonly gravel and cobbles, remaining after waves and currents have removed finer materials and transported them elsewhere.

Revetment A facing of stone, concrete, or other material to protect a scarp, embankment, or shore structure against erosion by waves or currents.

Rill marks Tiny drainage channels in a beach formed by the seaward flow of water.

Rip current A strong surface current flowing seaward, produced by the return flow of water transported to shore by waves and wind.

Ripple mark A small ridge of sand on the seabed produced by waves, wind, or currents, with crests less than 30 centimeters (one foot) apart and heights often less than 3.0 centimeters (0.1 foot).

Riprap A layer, facing, or protective mound of stones randomly placed to prevent erosion of an embankment or undermining of a structure; also the stone so used.

Scour The erosion of sedimentary material at the base of a shore structure by waves and currents.

Sediment The material deposited by water or wind.

Shoaling The propagation and transformation of waves in shallow water.

Shoreline The intersection of sea and land. The line delineating the shoreline on U.S. Coast and Geodetic Survey topographic maps is usually the mean high water line.

Shot rock Angular rock fragments produced by blasting in quarries.

Significant wave height The average height of the one-third highest waves of a wave group.

Significant wave period The estimated period of the one-third highest waves within a group.

Spit A point of land or a narrow shoal composed of loose sediment and projecting into a body of water.

Spring tide The highest and lowest tide levels that occur at the time of a new or full moon (about every two weeks), when the moon is aligned with the sun and the earth.

Still water level The elevation of the water surface when there are no waves.

Stockpile Sedimentary material placed on a beach to replenish it through natural longshore transport.

Storm surge A rise of water level on the coast, above the predicted tide, due to wind and barometric pressure on the water surface.

Surf zone The area between the outermost breakers and the shoreward limit of wave uprush.

Suspended load The material suspended in water and moved by waves and currents.

Swash mark The thin wavy line of fine sand, mica flakes, bits of seaweed, and other material left by wave uprush when it recedes from the beach.

Swell A group of long wind waves generated by a distant storm that has traveled far from its source; it has more regular and longer periods, and flatter crests than locally generated wind waves.

Tidal flats Marshy or muddy areas of the seabed which are covered and uncovered by the rise and fall of tidal water.

Tidal inlet A shallow inlet maintained by tidal currents.

Tidal range The difference in height between consecutive high and low waters.

Till Unstratified glacial drift composed of clay, sand, rocks, and gravel.

Tombolo A spit that connects an island to the mainland or to another island.

Updrift The direction opposite that of the predominant longshore movement (i.e., downdrift) of littoral materials.

Uplands Landforms adjacent to the coastline and above extreme high water level.

Water layer weathering Rock disintegration by chemical reactions with seawater and salt crystallization pressures.

Wave climate The prevailing wave characteristics (height, period, and frequency) and direction of wave approach at a coastal site.

Wave crest The top of a wave.

Wave cut platform A horizontal surface produced by wave erosion, usually below mean lower low water.

Wave diffraction The phenomenon by which wave energy passes around barriers (such as breakwaters and jetties) and through narrow openings to spread into sheltered areas.

Wave direction The direction from which waves approach an observer.

Wave group A series of waves in which the wave height, period, and direction are the same.

Wave height The vertical distance between adjacent wave crests and troughs.

Wave length The horizontal distance beteen adjacent wave crests.

Wave period Time between the passage of two successive wave crests.

Wave ray A line drawn perpendicular to wave crests, the direction of wave energy propagation.

Wave reflection Wave energy that is returned seaward when a wave strikes a steep beach or nearly vertical structure.

Wave refraction Changes in the direction of wave passage in shallow water.

Wave runup The rush of water up the face of a beach or structure produced by breaking waves. The maximum vertical height of water above still water level is the measure of runup.

Wave setup The accumulation of water in the surf zone and above the still water level produced by onshore transport in shoaling waves.

Wave spectrum A graph, table, or mathematical equation showing the distribution of wave energy as a function of wave frequency or period. A spectrum may be computed from wave measurements or predicted from wave theory.

Wave trough A shallow depression between successive wave crests; also that part of a wave below still water level.

Wetlands Shallow tidal flats or swamps that are inundated most of the time with fresh, brackish, or salt water.

Wind chop The steep and short-crested waves that are generated by a moderate breeze during the early growth of wind waves.

Wind waves Waves generated by the wind.

Bibliography

Ad Hoc Committee on Geologic Hazards. 1974. Meeting the geological hazard challenge. Report to the Washington State Legislature (1975 session). Olympia, Washington

Adee, B. H., E. P. Richey, and D. R. Christensen. 1976. Floating breakwater field assessment program, Friday Harbor, Washington. Coastal Engineering Research Center. Ft. Belvoir, Virginia. Technical Report 76-17.

Bagnold, R. A. 1954. Experiments on a gravity-free dispersion of large solid spheres in a Newtonian fluid under shear. *Proceedings of the Royal Society* (London), Ser. A, 225:49–63.

Bascom, W. N. 1951. The relationship between sand size and beach face shape. *Transactions of the American Geophysical Union*, 32:866–874.

Bortleson, G. C., M. J. Chrzastowski, and A. K. Helgerson. 1980. Historical changes of shoreline and wetland at eleven major deltas in the Puget Sound region, Washington. U.S. Geological Survey, Atlas HA–617.

Bretschneider, C. L. 1958. Revisions in wave forecasting: deep and shallow water. *Proceedings of the Sixth Conference on Coastal Engineering*. American Society of Civil Engineers. Pp. 30–67.

Brundage, W. L. Jr. 1960. Recent sediment of the Nisqually River delta, Puget Sound, Washington. Unpublished Master's Thesis. Seattle: University of Washington.

Clifton, H. E. 1969. Beach laminations: origin and nature. *Marine Geology*, 7(6):553–560.

Crosson, R. S. 1974. Compilation of earthquake hypocenters in Western Washington. State of Washington Department of Natural Resources, Information Circular 53. Olympia, Washington

de Jong, S. H. and H. F. W. Siebenhuener. 1972. Seasonal and secular variations of sea level on the Pacific coast of Canada. *The Canadian Surveyor*, 26(1):4–19.

Dean, R. G. 1978. Review of sediment transport relationships and the data base. *Proceedings of the Workshop on Coastal Sediment Transport*. Newark, Del.: University of Delaware Sea Grant. DEL-SG-15-78.

Dexter, R. N., D. E. Anderson, E. A. Quinlan, L. S. Goldstein, R. M. Strickland, R. M. Kocan, and M. Landolt. 1981. A summary of knowledge of Puget Sound related to chemical contaminants. Seattle, WA: National Oceanic and Atmospheric Administration, NOAA TM OMPA-13.

Ekman, M. R. 1978. Erosion control in a high energy coastal environment. American Society of Civil Engineers, Coastal Zone Conference, Volume III: 1680–1698.

Environment Canada. Waves recorded off Roberts Bank, B.C., Station 108, February 7, 1974 to April 3, 1976. Marine Environmental Data Service File 108-5. Ottawa, Canada.

———. Waves recorded off Sturgeon Bank, B.C., Station 102. Marine Environmental Data Service File 108-5.

———. Waves recorded off White Rock, B.C., Station 116. Marine Environmental Data Service File 108-5.

———. Waves recorded off Victoria, B.C., Station 4. Marine Environmental Data Service File 108-5.

Evans, L. 1932. Silt disposal at Nisqually Power Plant. *Western Construction Newsletter*, 7(24):725–726.

Galvin, C. J. 1972. A gross longshore transport rate formula. *Proceedings of the Thirteenth Conference on Coastal Engineering*. American Society of Civil Engineers. Pp. 953–970.

Gilbert, B. N. 1973. The potential of Puget Sound as a basin for the testing of models in a seaway. Unpublished Master's Thesis. Seattle: University of Washington.

Hand, B. M. 1967. Differentiation of beach and dune sands, using settling velocities of light and heavy minerals. *Journal of Sedimentary Petrology*, 37(2):514–520.

Harris, R. G. 1954. The surface winds over Puget Sound and the Strait of Juan de Fuca and their oceanographic effects. Unpublished Master's Thesis. Seattle: University of Washington.

Hayes, M. O. 1972. Forms of sediment accumulation in the beach zone. In: *Waves on beaches and resulting sediment transport* (R. E. Meyer, ed.). New York: Academic Press. Pp. 297–356.

Hicks, S. D. and J. E. Crosby. 1974. Trends and variability of yearly mean sea level. U.S. National Oceanographic and Atmospheric Administration Technical Memorandum, Number 5-13.

Hunter, R. E., H. E. Clifton, and R. L. Phillips. 1979. Depositional processes, sedimentary structures, and predicted vertical sequences in barred nearshore systems, southern Oregon coast. *Journal of Sedimentary Petrology*, 49(3):711–726.

Interagency Committee for Outdoor Recreation. 1974. Accretion beach inventory, Puget Sound, Hood Canal, San Juan Island, Strait of Juan de Fuca. Olympia, Washington.

James, W. R. 1974. Borrow material texture and beach fill stability. *Proceedings of the Fourteenth International Conference on Coastal Engineering*. American Society of Civil Engineers.

Keuler, R. F. 1979. Coastal zone processes and geomorphology of Skagit County, Washington. Unpublished Master's Thesis. Bellingham: Western Washington State University.

Knutson, P. L. 1980. Experimental dune restoration and stabilization, Nanset Beach, Cape Cod, Massachusetts. Coastal Engineering Research Center Technical Paper, Number 80-5.

———. 1977a. Planting guidelines for dune creation and stabilization. Coastal Engineering Research Center, Ft. Belvoir, Virginia. Technical Aid, Number 77-4.

———. 1977b. Planting guidelines for dune creation and stabilization. Coastal Engineering Research Center, Ft. Belvoir, Virginia. Technical Aid, Number 77-3.

Larsen, L. H. and D. R. Fenton. 1974. Observations of waves in the North Pacific. *Proceedings of the International Symposium on Ocean Wave Measurement and Analysis*. American Society of Civil Engineers, New Orleans, Louisiana, September 9–11, 1974. Pp. 197–213.

Laursen, E. M. 1958. The total sediment load of streams. *Journal of Hydraulics Division, Proceedings of the American Society of Civil Engineers* 84(HY1). Pp. 1530-1 to 1530-36.

Longuet-Higgins, M. S. and R. W. Stewart. 1964. Radiation stresses in water waves; a physical discussion, with applications. *Deep Sea Research*, 11:529–562.

Mathews, W. H., J. G. Fyles, and H. W. Nasmith. 1970. Postglacial crustal movements in southwestern British Columbia and adjacent Washington State. *Canadian Journal of Earth Science*, 7:690–702.

Maunder, W. J. 1968. Synoptic weather patterns in the Pacific Northwest. *Northwest Science*, 42(2):80–88.

McCrea, M. and J. H. Feldman. 1977. Interim assessment of Washington State shoreline management. *Coastal Zone Management Journal*, 3(2):119–150.

McGary, N. and J. H. Lincoln. 1977. *Tide prints. Surface tidal currents in Puget Sound*. Seattle, Washington: Washington Sea Grant. WSG 77-1.

Michel, W. H. 1968. Sea spectra simplified. *Proceedings of the April 1967 Meeting of the Gulf Section of the Society of Naval Architects and Marine Engineers*. Pp. 17–30.

Novak, I. D. 1972. Swash-zone competency of gravel-size sediment. *Marine Geology*, 13(5):335–346.

Plopper, C. S. 1979. Hydraulic sorting and longshore transport of beach sand, Pacific coast of Washington. Unpublished Dissertation. New York: Syracuse University.

Puget Sound Council of Governments. 1975. Regional disaster mitigation technical study for the Central Puget Sound region. Seattle, Washington.

Puget Sound Task Force of the Pacific Northwest River Basins Commission. 1970. Comprehensive study of water and related land resources. Puget Sound and adjacent waters.

Reed, R. J. 1980. Destructive winds caused by an orographically induced mesoscale cyclone. *Bulletin of the American Meteorological Society* 61(11):1346–1355.

Richey, E. P. 1978. Wind wave and boat wake analysis, Seacrest Marina, Seattle, Washington. Report prepared for the Port of Seattle.

Rubey, W. W. 1933. The size-distribution of heavy minerals within a water-laid sandstone. *Journal of Sedimentary Petrology*, 3(1):3–29.

Saville, T. Jr. 1954. The effect of fetch width on wave generation. U.S. Army Corps of Engineers, Beach Erosion Board, TM-70.

Schwartz, M. L. and G. F. Grabert. 1973. Coastal processes and prehistoric maritime cultures. In: *Coastal Geomorphology* (D. R. Coates, ed.).

Seymour, R. J. 1977. Estimating wave generation on restricted fetches. *Journal of Waterway, Port, Coastal and Ocean Division, American Society of Civil Engineers*, 103(WW2):251–264.

State of Washington Department of Fisheries. 1971. Criteria governing the design of bulkheads, land fills, and marinas in Puget Sound, Hood Canal, and Strait of Juan de Fuca for protection of fish and shellfish resources. Olympia, Washington.

State of Washington Department of Transportation. 1980. Hood Canal floating bridge, phase I report, Determination of the cause of failure. Olympia, Washington.

Sternberg, R. W. 1972. Predicting initial motion and bedload transport of sediment particles in the shallow marine environment. In: *Shelf sediment transport* (Swift, Duane, and Pilkey, eds.). Stroudsburg, PA: Dowden, Hutchinson & Ross, Inc. Pp. 61–82.

———. 1968. Friction factors in tidal channels with differing bed roughness. *Marine Geology*, 6:243–260.

———. 1967. Recent sediments in Bellingham Bay, Washington. *Northwest Science*, 41(2):63–79.

———. 1966. Boundary layer observations in a tidal current. *Journal of Geophysical Research*, 71(9):2175–2178.

Terich, T. A. 1978. Beach erosion protection in Puget Sound. American Society of Civil Engineers Coastal Zone Conference, Vol. III:1929–1936.

———. 1978. Puget Sound shore protection study. State of Washington Department of Ecology Report. Olympia, Washington.

Thorson, R. M. 1980. Ice-sheet glaciation of the Puget lowland, Washington, during the Vashon Stade (Late Pleistocene). *Quaternary Research*, 13:303–321.

———. 1979. Isostatic effects of the last glaciation in the Puget lowland, Washington. Unpublished Dissertation. Seattle: University of Washington.

Tubbs, D. W. 1975. Causes, mechanisms, and prediction of landsliding in Seattle. Unpublished Dissertation. Seattle: University of Washington.

———. 1974. Landslides in Seattle. State of Washington Department of Natural Resources, Division of Geology and Earth Resources Information Circular, Number 52.

U.S. Army Corps of Engineers. 1977. Permit program guide for applicants. Washington, D.C.: Department of the Army, Office of the Chief of Engineers. EP-1145-2-1.

———. 1977. Shore Protection Manual. Coastal Engineering Research Center. Ft. Belvoir, Virginia.

U.S. Army Corps of Engineers, Seattle District. 1979. Shoreline erosion control demonstration project, Oak Harbor, Washington (Section 54). 13 February 1979. Unpublished storm damage report.

———. 1978. Design memorandum, breakwater rehabilitation, Neah Bay, Washington.

———. 1976. General design memorandum, Ediz Hook beach erosion control.

———. 1975. Unpublished site condition report. Keystone Harbor, Island County, Washington.

———. 1971. Report on survey of Ediz Hook for beach erosion and related purposes. Port Angeles, Washington.

U.S. Army Corps of Engineers, North Pacific Division. 1971. Natural shoreline study, inventory report Columbia-North Pacific region, Washington and Oregon.

U.S. Coast and Geodetic Survey. 1948. Tidal current chart of Puget Sound, southern part.

U.S. Geological Survey. 1975. A study of earthquake losses in the Puget Sound, Washington, area. Open-File Report 75-375.

Vanicek, P. 1978. To the problem of noise reduction in sea-level records used in vertical crustal movement detection. *Physics of the Earth and Planetary Interiors*, 17:265–280.

Wigen, S.O. and F.E. Stephenson. 1980. Mean sea level on the Canadian west coast. *Proceedings of the 2nd Symposium on Problems Related to the Redefinition of North American Vertical Geodetic Networks*. Ottawa: Canadian Institute of Surveying. Pp. 107–124.

Index

Other Books in this Series

The Water Link: A History of Puget Sound as a Resource
Daniel Jack Chasan

Governing Puget Sound
Robert L. Bish

Marine Birds and Mammals of Puget Sound
Tony Angell and Kenneth C. Balcomb III

The Fertile Fjord: Plankton in Puget Sound
Richard M. Strickland